Pass

your Theory *and* Practical Driving Tests

Gavin Hoole and Clive Gibson

VELOCE PUBLISHING
THE PUBLISHER OF FINE AUTOMOTIVE BOOKS

Oxford
LEARNING

From the authors

Any examination can be a daunting affair and the driving tests are no exception. But the reward when you finally hold those car keys in your hand is a new and thrilling experience of freedom and independence.

Exam anxiety comes mainly from fear of the unknown, and fear of failure. This easy-to-use study manual will help you overcome both those fears. It gives you everything you need to prepare yourself well and eliminate the unknown, and it will help you to pass all the tests first time.

All the best!

First published in 2005 by

Veloce Publishing Limited, 33 Trinity Street, Dorchester DT1 1TT, England.
Fax: 01305 268864 E-mail: info@veloce.co.uk www.veloce.co.uk or www.velocebooks.com

and Oxford Learning Limited, Aristotle Lane, Oxford OX2 6TR, England.
Fax: 01865 517999 E-mail: info@odi-design.co.uk www.o-d-i.com/oxfordlearning

ISBN 1-904788-79-3/UPC 36847-00379-1

Readers with ideas for automotive books, or books on other transport or related hobby subjects, are invited to write to the editorial director of Veloce Publishing at the above address.

British Library Cataloguing in Publication Data – A catalogue record for this book is available from the British Library.

Editor: Gillian Somerscales
Cover photos: (left) © Bubbles/Lucy Tizard; (right) © Photodisc
Printed in the UK

Every effort has been made to ensure that the information contained in this publication is accurate at the time of going to press. The publishers cannot be held responsible for any inaccuracies. Information in this book is for guidance only.

Contents

Introduction

To drive unaccompanied on a public road in the UK you need to pass three tests:

▶ a THEORY TEST of your knowledge and understanding of all the rules and regulations concerning driving;

▶ a HAZARD PERCEPTION TEST of your ability to identify and respond to potential hazards on the road ahead; and

▶ a PRACTICAL DRIVING TEST of your driving skills and also of your application of the Theory and Hazard Perception Tests while driving.

This book has been carefully designed to help you prepare thoroughly for all three tests.

How to use this book

The book has been structured in a sequence and layout that make it easy for you to learn and remember what you need to know to pass the tests.

Test your own progress

Sets of multiple-choice questions are included at frequent intervals so that you can check your knowledge as you work your way through the book. The questions have been presented in a format similar to those you will have to answer in the official test at the Theory Test Centre, except that at the Centre the test appears on a computer screen.

After you complete each section of progress tests, check your answers against those given at the bottom of the page. If an answer you selected was wrong, make sure you understand why. Study that section of the chapter again to clarify your understanding before going on to the next section. Mark the page to come back to it again later to re-test yourself on that section.

Use the illustrations to help you learn

To help you remember the information and to ensure that learning with this book is enjoyable, drawings have been incorporated with the text. A ✓ in a drawing indicates a correct action while a ✗ indicates a wrong action.

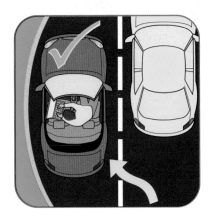

The all-in-one approach

During the Practical Driving Test, besides testing your driving skills, the examiner will also be marking you on how well you comply with all the rules and regulations you learnt for the Theory Test. To help you further with your preparation, the information on what you will have to do in the Practical Driving Test has been included with the relevant sections of the Theory Test information, shown separately in special orange-tinted panels headed with a car symbol. So, as you prepare for the Theory Test, you will also see what the examiner will be testing during your Practical Driving Test – the particular driving skill, and also your application of the Highway Code. This will help you to understand how the two tests fit together, and will give you a more complete view of how to become a licensed driver. Your preparation for the tests will therefore be that much easier.

 Sample

These panels contain specific information about what the examiner will ask you to do in the Practical Driving Test.

▶ Remember to read these panels as you work through the theory.

Important – study everything in the book

The official Theory Test consists of a selection of 35 questions drawn randomly from a battery of several hundred questions. This book provides all the information you need to answer all the questions you may be asked. There are test questions on almost every single line of text in this book, from Chapter 4 onwards. So learn all the information from Chapter 4 to the end; no unnecessary information has been included.

We hope that you will learn the information not only in order to pass the tests, but also so that you can become a responsible and safe driver on our roads.

2 Licensed to drive

The Highway Code spells out the rules and regulations for driving on public roads – the dos and don'ts of safe driving. The Code exists for the protection of all road users, and all drivers must comply with these rules and regulations. Its content relating to drivers is comprehensively covered in this book from Chapter 4 onwards. The Theory Test and the Practical Driving Test have been devised to test knowledge, understanding and practical application of these rules and regulations before new drivers are allowed to drive on public roads.

Overview of the Theory Test

What the Theory Test includes

The Theory Test covers the following areas:

- road traffic regulations and traffic signs;
- driver behaviour on the road;
- driving in different road and traffic conditions;
- other road users and the risks involved;
- general rules, regulations and safety matters;
- road and vehicle safety;
- environmental matters.

The test consists of two elements:

- a computer-based test of 35 multiple-choice questions that must be answered in 40 minutes;
- a Hazard Perception (HP) test that must be completed in 20 minutes.

You can expect to have your results within about 30 minutes of finishing the test. You must pass both elements. If you fail one of them you will need to apply to do the whole Theory Test again. You must wait a minimum of three clear working days before you can take the Theory Test again.

The multiple-choice test

You will be told how to complete the test on the computer, and given an opportunity to practise answering questions before the actual test begins.

Some questions require you to select more than one answer, so read the instructions for each question carefully. You will be able to move backwards and forwards through the questions and change your answers if you want to. You must answer 30 of the 35 questions correctly in order to pass.

The test is available in several foreign languages. Check with your local testing centre and, if your language is not one of these, ask if you may take an interpreter with you. If you are disabled or dyslexic, phone 0870 010 1372 (0845 600 6700 in Northern Ireland) to make special arrangements to do the test.

You may be exempted from doing a Theory Test if you are upgrading your licence category. Check with your local testing authority to find out whether you qualify for exemption.

1 Which of the following apply? (2)

a Tyres should be inflated above normal pressure when driving short distances. ☐

b Under-inflated tyres can cause heavy steering. ☐

c Under-inflated tyres reduce fuel consumption. ☐

d Tyres should be inflated above normal pressure when driving fast. ☐

The Hazard Perception Test

You will be allowed to take a break of a few minutes, if you wish, after completing the Theory Test before starting the HP test.

You will be shown how to complete the HP test, and will be given a few practice opportunities.

The HP test consists of a series of video clips of driving scenes from a driver's viewpoint. Each clip shows one or more hazards developing on the road ahead. As soon as you see the hazard developing, press the relevant button. The sooner you respond to each situation, the higher your score will be.

To pass, you must score the required number of marks for the HP test applicable to the category of licence you are applying for (e.g. car, motorcycle, etc.).

Overview of the Practical Driving Test

The normal test will last about 40 minutes. If you are requalifying after having been convicted of a serious driving offence, you will have to do an extended test that will last about 70 minutes.

If you pass the test using an automatic vehicle, you will be licensed to drive an automatic vehicle and this licence will act as a provisional licence to drive a manual car.

Vehicle requirements

The vehicle that you practise in must be suitably insured for you to drive, and if the same vehicle is used for the driving test, it must also:

- ▶ be mechanically sound;
- ▶ be legally roadworthy with a current MOT certificate, if necessary;
- ▶ display a valid tax disc, unless exempt;
- ▶ display L-plates (D-plates in Wales) front and rear, but not in any windows (these plates must be covered up when the vehicle is not being driven by a learner driver);
- ▶ have a fully functional seatbelt for the front passenger seat;
- ▶ have a head restraint (not a clip-on) on the front passenger seat;
- ▶ have an additional interior rear view mirror for use by the examiner;
- ▶ not be fitted with a spare wheel meant for temporary use;
- ▶ be suitable for the test. Unsuitable vehicles include:
  – vehicles with no clear view to the rear, other than via exterior mirrors;
  – vehicles with only a driver's seat;
  – vehicles with more than eight passenger seats;
  – loaded or partly loaded vehicles;
  – vehicles in excess of 3.5 tonnes in weight;
  – vehicles towing a trailer.

If any of these requirements is not met, the test will be cancelled and you will lose the fee.

What the Practical Driving Test includes

During the Practical Driving Test you will have to:

▶ pass an eyesight test;

▶ demonstrate good general driving ability;

▶ perform any two of the following:
  – reversing around a corner;
  – turning in the road;
  – reverse parking;

▶ perform an emergency stop, if asked;

▶ demonstrate that
  – you can drive safely;
  – you can complete a set of driving exercises;
  – you have a thorough knowledge of the Highway Code.

The following sections set out in more detail the knowledge that the examiner will expect you to have gained by the time you take the Practical Driving Test.

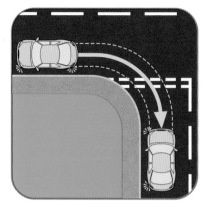

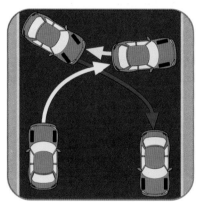

Vehicle controls, equipment and components

You must show that you:

▶ understand the function of, and can use competently, the
  – accelerator;   – clutch;   – gears;
  – footbrake;   – handbrake;   – steering wheel;

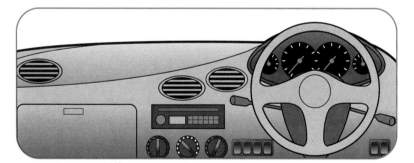

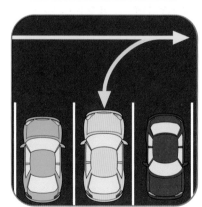

▶ know the function of other controls and switches in the car that have a bearing on road safety, and are able to use them competently;

▶ understand the meaning of the gauges and other displays on the instrument panel;

▶ know the legal requirements for the vehicle;

▶ are able to carry out routine safety checks on:
  – oil and coolant levels;
  – tyre pressures;

▶ are able to identify defects with the
  – steering;   – brakes;
  – tyres;   – seatbelts;
  – lights;   – reflectors;
  – direction indicators; – windscreen wipers and washers;
  – horn;   – rear view mirrors;
  – speedometer;   – exhaust system;

▶ understand the effect that a loaded roof rack or extra passengers will have on the handling of your vehicle.

Road-user behaviour

You must be aware of:

▶ the most common causes of accidents;

▶ which road users are most at risk and how to reduce that risk;

▶ the rules, risks and effects of drinking and driving;

▶ the effect of fatigue, illness and drugs on driving performance;

▶ age-related risks associated with other road users, especially children, teenagers and the elderly;

▶ the likely actions of other road users, and what appropriate precautions to take;

▶ the essential part played by courtesy and consideration towards other road users in safe driving.

Vehicle characteristics

You must know:

▶ the principles concerning braking distances and road holding under various road and weather conditions;

▶ the handling characteristics of other vehicles with regard to stability, speed, braking and manoeuvrability;

▶ that some vehicles are less easily seen than others;

▶ how to assess the risks caused by other vehicles and suggest precautions that can be taken, for example in relation to:
  – large commercial vehicles moving to the right before turning left;
  – blind spots for some commercial vehicle drivers;
  – bicycles, motorcycles and large vehicles being buffeted by strong winds.

Road and weather conditions

You must:

▶ know the hazards likely to occur in both daylight and the dark, and on different types of road, for example on:
  – single carriageways, including country lanes;
  – three-lane roads;
  – dual carriageways and motorways;

▶ know which road surfaces provide the better or poorer grip when braking;

▶ know the hazards caused by bad weather, for example:
  – rain;
  – fog;
  – snow;
  – ice;
  – strong winds;

▶ have gained driving experience on urban and higher-speed roads (but not motorways) in both daylight and the dark;

▶ be able to assess the risks caused by road and traffic conditions, to judge how the conditions may cause others to drive unsafely, and to take appropriate precautions.

Traffic signs, rules, and regulations

▶ You must have a sound knowledge of the meaning of traffic signs and road markings, for example:
  – speed limits;
  – parking restrictions;
  – zebra and pelican crossings.

Vehicle control and road procedure

You must have the knowledge and skills required to carry out various tasks safely and competently, practising the proper use of mirrors, observation and signals.

  You must be able to do the following:

▶ take necessary precautions before getting in or out of the vehicle;

▶ before starting the engine, carry out safety checks on the
  – doors;
  – seat and head restraints;
  – seat belts;
  – mirrors;

▶ check that the handbrake is on and the gear lever is in neutral before starting the engine;

▶ start the engine and move off:
  – straight ahead and at an angle;
  – on the level, uphill and downhill;

▶ select the correct road position for normal driving;

▶ use proper observation in all traffic conditions;

▶ drive at a speed suitable for road and traffic conditions;

▶ react promptly to all risks;

▶ change traffic lanes safely;

▶ pass stationary vehicles safely;

▶ meet, overtake and cross the path of oncoming vehicles;

▶ turn right and left at junctions, including crossroads and roundabouts;

▶ drive ahead at crossroads and roundabouts;

▶ keep a safe following distance when travelling behind other traffic;

▶ act correctly at pedestrian crossings;

▶ show proper regard for the safety of other road users, with particular care towards the most vulnerable;

▶ drive on urban and rural roads and, where possible, dual carriageways, keeping up with the flow of traffic where it is safe and proper to do so;

▶ comply with traffic regulations and traffic signals given by the police, traffic wardens and other road users;

▶ stop the vehicle safely, normally and in an emergency, without locking the wheels;

▶ turn the vehicle in the road to face the opposite way using the forward and reverse gears;

▶ reverse the vehicle into a side road, keeping reasonably close to the kerb;

- park parallel to the kerb while driving in a reverse gear;
- park the vehicle in a multi-storey car park or other parking bay, on the level, uphill and downhill, in both forward and reverse directions;
- cross all types of railway level crossing.

Additional knowledge

You must know:

- the importance of correct tyre pressures;
- the action needed to avoid and correct skids;
- how to drive through floods and flooded areas;
- what to do if you are involved in an accident or breakdown, including the special arrangements for accidents or breakdowns on a motorway;
- basic first aid for use on the road;
- what action to take to deter car thieves.

Driving on motorways

You must gain a sound knowledge of the special rules, regulations and driving techniques for motorway driving before taking your driving test.

After you have passed your test, you are advised to take a few lessons with an Approved Driving Instructor (ADI) before driving unsupervised on motorways.

Pass marks

You will pass the Practical Driving Test if you don't commit a Serious or Dangerous fault, or more than 15 Less-serious Driving faults, during the test. When you have passed, you may drive without L- or D-plates, unsupervised, and also on motorways.

Driving test for towing trailers or caravans

You must achieve everything in the overview of the practical driving test, except items that clearly don't apply to you. In particular, you should know how to do the following:

- turn a vehicle and trailer to travel in the opposite direction without reversing, where possible, for example, using a roundabout or side roads;
- stop the vehicle and trailer as quickly as possible, safely and under full control;
- reverse the towing vehicle and trailer:
  – under control;
  – with effective observation;
  – on a predetermined course;
  – to enter a restricted opening; and
  – to stop so that the extreme rear of the trailer is within a clearly defined area;

THE ROAD AHEAD

- select a safe and suitable place to stop the vehicle and trailer reasonably close to the nearside kerb when required:
  – on the level;
  – facing uphill;
  – facing downhill;
  – before reaching a parked vehicle, but leaving sufficient room to move away again;
- use additional extension mirrors for thorough observation to compensate for the restricted view caused by large trailers and caravans;
- show consideration for other road users by pulling over safely when necessary, to avoid the build-up of queues of following traffic;
- uncouple and couple the trailer from the towing vehicle safely.

Uncoupling

You must:

- select a safe place with firm and level ground;
- ensure that the brakes are applied on both the towing vehicle and the trailer;
- ensure that the wheels, legs or other devices provided for supporting the trailer after uncoupling are lowered correctly, and that strong planks or metal load spreaders are used to distribute the weight if there is any risk of the legs sinking into the ground;
- disconnect the electric line(s) and stow them away safely, remove any chain or coupling, and manoeuvre the trailer clear of the towing hook;
- remove any fitted stabilizing equipment and the trailer number plate, where appropriate.

Coupling up

You must:

- ensure that the brakes are correctly applied on the trailer;
- manoeuvre the towing vehicle so that the trailer may be safely and easily coupled to it;
- attach the vehicle to the towing vehicle securely;
- attach any safety chain or device and the electrical connections;
- correctly fit any stabilizing equipment;
- connect the electric line(s);
- ensure that the wheels, legs or other devices provided for supporting the trailer are raised and secured correctly;
- check that the coupling is secure by using a method appropriate to the vehicle and trailer;
- check the operation of all lights and the fitting of the correct number plate, where appropriate;
- release the trailer brake, having ensured that the handbrake on the towing vehicle is on.

3 Applying for the tests

The five-step process

There are five key steps to obtaining a full driving licence:
1. Apply for a provisional driving licence.
2. Make a booking for the Theory Test, and pass the test.
3. Arrange driving lessons.
4. Make a booking for the Practical Driving Test.
5. Take the Practical Driving Test, and pass the test.

Step 1: Applying for a provisional driving licence

To apply for a provisional licence, complete the application **forms DL1** and **DL750**, available from any Post Office, and (if living in Northern Ireland) also the **DL1** from Driver and Vehicle Licensing Northern Ireland.

Requirements

▷ Enclose two passport-size photographs when you submit the forms.

▷ To take the test, you must be 'normally resident' in the UK.

▷ The minimum age at which you may start driving is 17 years. For people receiving a Disability Allowance at the higher rate, the age is 16 years.

▷ You must have a valid, signed provisional driving licence in order to drive on the road, even as a learner driver.

▷ If you have had surgery to correct your eyesight, you must declare this when you apply for your provisional licence.

Enquiries

Contact the Driver and Vehicle Licensing Agency on **0870 240 0009** for any further information.

Step 2: Booking the Theory Test

There are four ways to make a booking:

▷ Telephone: 0870 010 1372 (0845 600 6700 in Northern Ireland);

▷ Internet: www.driving-tests.co.uk or www.motoring.gov.uk

▷ By post: Driving Standards Agency or Driver and Vehicle Testing Agency, PO Box 148, Salford M5 3SY

▷ In person at your nearest local booking office.

To cancel or postpone a booking, notify the booking office at least three days before the test, otherwise you will lose your fee.

What to take to the Theory Test

You must have the following original documents in order to take the test:

▷ your signed provisional driving licence and photographic identification (e.g. passport/student union card), or

▷ your signed photo-card licence and paper counterpart.

THE ROAD AHEAD

Step 3: Arranging driving lessons

Approved Driving Instructors (ADIs) are registered with the DSA and are fully qualified. You are advised to use an ADI to teach you to drive. Ask your friends and relatives to recommend a good ADI.

Legal requirements

To learn to drive you must:

▶ be at least 17 years old (if you receive the higher mobility component of the Disability Living Allowance (DLA) for a disability you may start driving at 16);

▶ be able to read in good daylight (with glasses or contact lenses, if you wear them) a motor vehicle number plate with letters 79.4 mm (3.1 in.) high 20.5 metres (about 67 feet) away; number plates with a narrower font, such as the new-style number plates introduced during 2001, should be readable from a distance of 20 metres (66 feet);

▶ be medically fit to drive;

▶ hold a provisional driving licence for a car, or a full licence for another category of vehicle;

▶ ensure that the vehicle being driven is legally roadworthy, has a current MOT certificate if it is over the prescribed age, and displays a valid tax disc;

▶ make sure that the vehicle is properly insured for its use;

▶ display L-plates (or, if you wish, D-plates in Wales) on the front and rear of the vehicle;

▶ be supervised by a person who:
  – has held for at least three years (and still holds) a full EC/EEA licence for the category of vehicle driven;
  – is at least 21 years old;

▶ wear a seatbelt, unless granted an exemption, and ensure that all the seatbelts in the vehicle, and their anchorages and fitting, are free from obvious defects;

▶ ensure that children under 14 years carried in the vehicle are suitably restrained by the appropriate restraint or an adult seatbelt;

▶ be aware of the legal requirements for notifying medical conditions that could affect safe driving. If a vehicle has been adapted for a disability, ensure that all the adaptations are suitable for controlling the vehicle safely;

▶ know the rules in respect of the issue, presentation and display of:
  – driving licences;
  – insurance certificates;
  – tax discs.

When learning to drive a category B+E combination, that is a light vehicle towing a trailer, you must comply with the requirements of a provisional licence. In particular, you should:

▶ display L-plates (or, if you wish, D-plates in Wales) on the front and rear of the unit;

▶ be supervised by a person who is at least 21 years old and has a current licence for category B+E that they have held for at least three years.

Step 4: Booking the Practical Driving Test

Complete application **form DL26**, obtainable from any **DSA Driving Test Centre**. Details of fees can be obtained at your nearest driving test centre or phone **0870 010 1372**. Fees can be paid by cheque, postal order or credit card.

You should apply well before the time, and give your preferred date and any special circumstances. Send the completed form to the address shown on the back. If you need to postpone the test appointment, tell the DSA at least 11 clear working days beforehand, otherwise you will lose your fee.

Step 5: Taking the Practical Driving Test

What to take with you

You must take your **provisional driving licence** and your **Theory Test pass certificate** with you when you arrive to do the Practical Driving Test. If you have a photo-licence you must take the **counterpart** with you as well. It is part of the licence. You must have some form of **photographic identification** and all the documents must be **original**, not photocopies.

Your instructor, or a friend, may accompany you during the test but may not take any part in it.

Let the preparation begin!

Remember, all the information given in this book from Chapter 4 onwards applies to both tests. Specific information and guidelines for the Practical Driving Test are provided in the orange-tinted panels in the appropriate section.

It's now time to start gaining the knowledge you will need for taking the multiple-choice Theory Test and Hazard Perception Test, and the Practical Driving Test.

4 Your responsibilities as a driver

Most accidents are the result of driver error. Sometimes an accident happens because the driver's ability was impaired through illness, drugs or alcohol. Sometimes it is caused by poor driver attitude, or lack of alertness or concentration.

As a driver, you must ensure that you meet the requirements with regard to health and fitness, and also that you have all the documentation required for yourself and for your vehicle.

Fitness and health

▶ You must be medically fit to drive. If you're not sure about your medical fitness, ask your doctor (see also 'Vision' opposite).

▶ You must tell the Driver and Vehicle Licensing Agency (DVLA) about any health condition that could affect your driving.

Alertness

▶ Look out for the signals of other road users, and proceed only when it is clearly safe to do so.

▶ Be careful of indicators on other vehicles that may not have been cancelled.

▶ If you feel tired, don't drive for longer than one hour at a time.

▶ If you feel sleepy:
  – open your window for fresh air;
  – stop in a safe place to rest – not on the hard shoulder of a motorway; then

– if possible, snooze for 15 minutes; or
– have some strong coffee.

▶ On a motorway, if you decide to rest, leave at the next exit or service area.

▶ If possible, don't make long journeys between midnight and 6 am.

▶ Plan for a 15-minute break after every two hours of driving.

15 mins

2 hrs

🚗 Alertness

Awareness and anticipation

The examiner will be observing your awareness, and evaluating how well you anticipate possible dangers and consider other road users.

Things you must do

▶ Look out for other road users and try to anticipate their actions.

▶ Predict how their actions will affect you.

▶ React safely and in good time.

Pedestrians

▶ Give way to pedestrians when turning from one road into another.

▶ Take extra care when there are young, elderly or disabled pedestrians about.

Cyclists

▶ Look out for cyclists when crossing bus and cycle lanes.

▶ Look out for cyclists overtaking on your left.

▶ Take extra care when there are child cyclists about.

Motorcyclists

▶ Look out for motorcycles in slow-moving traffic.

▶ Look out for motorcycles overtaking on your left.

▶ Look out for motorcycles at junctions.

Animals

▶ Take extra care when there are animals about.

▶ Allow horse-riders and other animal handlers plenty of room.

▶ Take extra care when there are young horse-riders about.

▶ Plan your approach carefully and stop if necessary.

Emergency vehicles

▶ When you hear an emergency vehicle, establish from which direction it is coming.

▶ Try to move out of its way.

▶ If necessary, pull over and stop if it is safe to do so.

Some don'ts

▶ Don't react suddenly to road and traffic conditions.

▶ Don't become irritated with other road users.

▶ Don't sound your horn aggressively.

▶ Don't rev the engine or edge forward to intimidate pedestrians.

Maintaining concentration

▶ Don't lose your concentration by:
  – reading or looking at a map while driving;
  – fiddling with the radio or CD player;
  – listening to loud music that can drown out other sounds;

  – using a mobile phone;
  – using a hands-free phone system;
  – talking into a microphone;
  – getting engrossed in discussions or arguments;
  – eating or drinking;
  – applying make-up;
  – using an electric shaver.

▶ Don't have windscreen stickers, or objects hanging from the mirror, as these can restrict your view and distract your attention.

▶ Avoid using hands-free communications equipment while driving.

▶ If communication is essential, stop and park at a suitable and safe place before using such equipment.

▶ To avoid being distracted, don't use the following while driving:
  – route guidance and navigation systems;
  – congestion warning systems;
  – computers;
  – multi-media equipment.

 Maintaining concentration

The examiner will be watching your ability to maintain concentration while driving.

Vision

▶ Ensure that you are able to read a standard vehicle number plate from 20.5 metres away in clear daylight, and a new-style number plate from 20 metres away.

▶ If you can do this only when wearing glasses or contact lenses, then they must be worn at all times while driving and when doing the practical test.

▶ If you don't have your glasses that you need for driving, don't drive; use an alternative means of transport.

▶ Don't wear tinted glasses, lenses or visors when driving at night or in poor visibility.

 Vision

The examiner will begin the test by asking you to read the number plate on a car parked nearby. If you are not able to do this you will fail and the test will be stopped. Those people who have difficulty speaking English can write down what they see.

Alcohol and drugs

▶ Don't drink and drive.

▶ You must not drive with:
  – a breath alcohol level more than 35 μg/100 ml, or
  – a blood alcohol level more than 80 mg/100 ml.

▶ Alcohol gives the driver:
  – a false sense of confidence;
  – reduced concentration and co-ordination;
  – slower reaction time;
  – impaired judgement of speed, distance and risk;
  – reduced ability to control the vehicle and drive safely.

▶ Because these effects can last for eight hours or more, arrange alternative transport if you are going to drink.

▶ Don't drive under the influence of narcotic drugs or medicine.

▶ The combined use of alcohol and drugs can result in fatal or serious accidents.

▶ If you need to take any medicine, ask your doctor or pharmacist, or read the label, about the effects it may have. It may affect your driving ability.

Alcohol and drugs

Don't arrive at the test centre smelling of alcohol or drugs.

Before driving

▶ Plan your route and set aside enough time for the journey.

▶ Make sure you understand each of the warning displays on the vehicle instrument panel.

Handbrake on

Headlights on full beam

Fault in the braking system

Hazard warning flashers are switched on

Left indicator is flashing

Right indicator is flashing

▶ In winter, check the local weather forecast for ice and snow on the way.

▶ Wear appropriate clothing that does not interfere with your control of the vehicle.

▶ Wear suitable shoes that allow you to maintain control of the pedals.

▶ Ensure that you are familiar with the vehicle's controls and how they work.

▶ Adjust the mirrors and seat to ensure full control, comfort and maximum vision.

▶ Adjust the head restraint to protect your neck from injury in the event of an accident.

▶ Make sure you have enough fuel for the journey.

Before driving

Pre-trip inspection

In the presence of the examiner, *before starting the engine*, you must check the interior of the vehicle to ensure that it is ready for the test to commence.

Things you must do

▶ Check that all the doors are properly closed.

▶ Check that the handbrake is applied.

▶ Check that the gear lever is in neutral, or **N** or **P** in an automatic vehicle.

▶ Adjust the driver's seat to suit your needs.

▶ Check that the head restraints are secure and properly adjusted.

▶ Adjust the rear view mirrors to suit your needs.

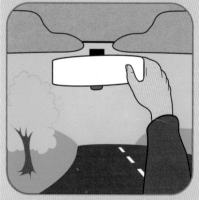

▶ Strap on the seatbelt and make sure that it is comfortable and secure.

Your responsibilities as a driver

The number in brackets at the end of each question indicates how many correct answers you should mark.

1 Which of the following apply? (3)

a You must be medically fit to drive. ☑

b You must tell the Driver and Vehicle Licensing Agency about any health condition that could affect your driving. ☑

c Proceed only when it is clearly safe to do so. ☑

d Plan a 15-minute break every 4 hours. ☐

2 What should you do if you feel sleepy? (2)

a Open your window for fresh air. ☑

b Smoke something. ☐

c Close your eyes briefly when on a straight open road. ☐

d Have some strong coffee. ☑

3 Which of the following statements are correct? (2)

a Leave a motorway at an exit or service area. ☑

b Don't make long journeys between midnight and 6 am. ☑

c You may pick up hikers on a motorway. ☐

d You may use a mobile phone while driving. ☐

4 Which of the following could affect your concentration while driving? (2)

a Getting involved in an argument. ☑

b Looking out for the signals of other road users. ☐

c Looking at a road map. ☑

d Giving way to horse-riders. ☐

5 Which of the following apply while driving? (2)

a You may use hand-held communications equipment. ☐

b Don't have objects hanging from the mirror. ☑

c Drive on the right-hand side of the roadway. ☐

d Don't use multi-media equipment. ☑

6 At what distance should you be able to read a standard new-style vehicle number plate? (1)

a 19 metres. ☐

b 20.5 metres. ☐

c 21 metres. ☐

d 20 metres. ☑

7 Which of the following apply while driving? (2)

a Don't wear tinted glasses at night. ☑

b Set aside enough time for a journey. ☑

c Alcohol makes you more alert. ☐

d The effect of alcohol lasts up to four hours. ☐

8 You must not drive under the following circumstances: (1)

a With a breath alcohol level more than 25 µg/100 ml. ☐

b With a breath alcohol level more than 35 µg/100 ml. ☑

c With a breath alcohol level more than 45 µg/100 ml. ☐

d With a breath alcohol level more than 55 µg/100 ml. ☐

9 You must not drive with a blood alcohol level more than: (1)

a 60 mg/100 ml. ☐

b 70 mg/100 ml. ☐

c 80 mg/100 ml. ☑

d 85 mg/100 ml. ☐

10 Which of the following are true? (2)

a You may drive under the influence of narcotics only under certain circumstances. ☐

b The effects of alcohol can last for eight hours or more. ☑

c The use of alcohol and drugs can result in serious accidents. ☑

d Alcohol improves concentration. ☐

11 Which of the following apply before driving? (2)

a Make sure you have enough fuel for the journey. ☑

b Check the local weather forecast in summer. ☐

c Adjust the neck restraint to protect your head from injury. ☑

d Consume a small amount of alcohol to improve your reaction time. ☐

12 Which of the following apply before driving? (2)

a Ensure that you are familiar with the vehicle's controls. ☑

b Wait till you're driving before adjusting the mirrors. ☐

c Wait till you're driving before adjusting the seat. ☐

d Wear clothing that does not interfere with your control of the vehicle. ☑

YOU AND YOUR VEHICLE

12 a, d	11 a, c	10 b, c	9 c	8 b	7 a, b
6 d	5 b, d	4 a, c	3 a, b	2 a, d	1 a, b, c

Attitude and consideration

▶ If you are angry, calm down before you start to drive.

▶ Don't drive dangerously.

▶ Drive with due care and attention.

▶ Always drive with reasonable consideration for other road users.
  – Be understanding of other drivers who may cause problems.
  – Be patient with other drivers' mistakes and try not to react.

▶ Stay calm at all times.

▶ When feeling agitated, move over, stop, and relax before continuing.

▶ Don't over-react if a vehicle recklessly moves into your path. Adjust to a safe following distance, and get on with driving normally.

 Attitude and consideration

The examiner will be watching your attitude towards other road users and the consideration you show them.

Penalty point system

The penalty point system aims at deterring drivers from driving badly or dangerously. If you are found violating a road traffic law or driving badly, penalty points will be recorded against you.

The accumulation of just a few penalty points can result in imprisonment, a large fine and prohibition from driving for a minimum of 12 months. In some cases your vehicle could also be confiscated.

Courts are obliged to endorse penalty points on a licence, depending on the nature of the offence. Examples of penalties are included in the table opposite.

Your licence will be revoked if your penalty points reach 6 or more as a result of offences you have committed during your first two years of driving. You will then have to re-take your theory and practical tests, and re-apply for your provisional licence.

Driving under the influence of alcohol

▶ Any driver may be disqualified for:
  – driving under the influence of alcohol; or
  – having more than twice the legal limit of alcohol in breath or blood; or
  – refusing to provide a specimen.

▶ If this should happen twice within a period of eleven years, the driver must also satisfy the Driver and Vehicle Licensing Agency (DVLA) Medical Branch that they do not have an alcohol problem and are fit to drive before their licence may returned to them after their period of disqualification has ended.

▶ Persistent use of drugs or alcohol could result in your driving licence being withdrawn.

Penalty table

Offence	Maximum penalties			
	Prison	Fine	Disqualification	Penalty points
*Causing death by dangerous driving	10 years	Unlimited	Obligatory 2 years minimum	3–11 (if exceptionally not disqualified)
Causing death by careless driving under the influence of drink or drugs	10 years	Unlimited	Obligatory 2 years minimum	3–11 (if exceptionally not disqualified)
*Dangerous driving	2 years	Unlimited	Obligatory	3–11 (if exceptionally not disqualified)
Careless or inconsiderate driving		£2500	Discretionary	3–9
Driving while unfit through drink or drugs or with excess alcohol; or failing to provide a specimen for analysis	6 months	£5000	Obligatory	3–11 (if exceptionally not disqualified)
Failing to stop after an accident or failing to report an accident	6 months	£5000	Discretionary	5–10
Driving when disqualified	6 months (12 months in Scotland)	£5000	Discretionary	6
Driving after refusal or revocation of licence on medical grounds	6 months	£5000	Discretionary	3–6
Driving without insurance	—	£5000	Discretionary	6–8
Driving otherwise than in accordance with a licence	—	£1000	Discretionary	3–6
Speeding	—	£1000 (£2500 for motorway offences)	Discretionary	3–6 or 3 (fixed penalty)
Traffic light offences	—	£1000	Discretionary	3
No MOT certificate	—	£1000	—	—
Seatbelt offences	—	£500	—	—
Failing to identify driver of a vehicle		£1000	Discretionary	3

* Where a court disqualifies a person on conviction for one of these offences, it must order an extended re-test. The courts also have discretion to order a re-test for any other offence which carries penalty points: an extended re-test where disqualification is obligatory, and an ordinary test where disqualification is not obligatory.

YOU AND YOUR VEHICLE

Document requirements

- You should carry your documents with you at all times. If you are not able to produce them when asked to do so, they must be produced at a police station within seven days (five days in Northern Ireland).
- All vehicles on the road must have a valid Vehicle Excise Duty disc (tax disc) displayed at all times on the bottom left-hand side of the windscreen.
- Any vehicle exempt from duty must display a NIL licence.

Items you should carry with you

Driving licence, vehicle registration document, insurance certificate, MOT certificate.

Supervising a learner driver

- To supervise a learner driver you must:
  - have held a full licence for 3 years;
  - be at least 21 years old.

Licences

- In order to drive legally, a learner driver must have a signed, valid provisional licence to drive on the road.
- All vehicles used on the road must have a vehicle registration document that specifies:
  - the date of first registration;
  - the registration number;
  - the previous keeper;
  - the registered keeper;
  - the make of the vehicle;
  - the engine size and chassis number;
  - the year of manufacture;
  - the colour.
- You must inform the Driver and Vehicle Licensing Agency (the DVLA) in Swansea when:
  - you buy or sell a vehicle;
  - you change your name or permanent address;
  - your health adversely affects your driving;
  - your eyesight does not meet the required standard.
- You must notify the licensing authority immediately when you purchase a second-hand vehicle.

Insurance

- To be legal, vehicles must have a minimum of third party insurance that covers:
  - injury to another person;
  - damage to someone's property;
  - damage to other vehicles, but not yours.
- You must produce your motor insurance certificate:
  - when requested to do so by a police officer;
  - when taxing your vehicle.

- In the event of an insurance claim, you must pay the first amount (or 'excess') of any claim.
- Before driving someone else's vehicle, you must make sure that it is insured for your use.
- The cost of insurance may be reduced if:
  - you are older than 25 years;
  - you complete a Pass Plus training scheme. (Enquire at your testing centre.)
- A temporary insurance certificate is known as a cover note.

MOT certificate

- Motor cars must have an MOT certificate once they are three years old.
- An MOT certificate is normally valid for one year after the date it was issued, so it must be renewed annually.
- The vehicle must have an MOT certificate in order to renew the road tax disc.
- If you drive a car without an MOT certificate, this could invalidate the insurance.
- It is legal to drive a car without an MOT certificate when you are taking it for an appointment at an MOT centre.
- An MOT certificate is not required by
  - a small trailer;
  - a caravan.

Your responsibilities as a driver continued

The number in brackets at the end of each question indicates how many correct answers you should mark.

13 Which of the following are correct? (2)

a Remember to tip parking attendants before leaving your vehicle in a car park.

b If angry, calm down before driving.

c Be understanding of other drivers.

d Give way to hot air balloons crossing the road overhead.

14 Which of the following statements are correct? (2)

a A few penalty points can result in imprisonment.

b A few penalty points can result in a large fine.

c You need many penalty points for your vehicle to be confiscated.

d You need many penalty points to be disqualified from driving.

15 How many penalty points during the first two years of driving can result in your licence being revoked? (1)

a 4.

b 5.

c 6.

d 7.

16 Under what circumstances may a driver be disqualified? (2)

a Having the smell of alcohol on your breath while driving.

b Having just less than the legal limit of alcohol in the breath or blood.

c Refusing to provide a breath or blood specimen.

d Driving under the influence of alcohol.

17 If asked to produce the required driving documents how long do you have to do so? (1)

a 7 days (5 in Northern Ireland).

b 5 days (7 in Northern Ireland).

c 48 hours.

d 8 days.

18 The Vehicle Excise Duty disc must be displayed on the windscreen: (1)

a Top left.

b Top right.

c Bottom left.

d Bottom right.

19 To supervise a learner driver you must: (2)

a Have held a full licence for three years.

b Be at least 21 years old.

c Have a valid provisional licence.

d Inform the DVLA of your intentions.

20 You must tell the Driver and Vehicle Licensing Agency: (2)

a The name of the previous keeper of the vehicle.

b The engine size and chassis number.

c When you buy or sell a vehicle.

d When your health adversely affects your driving.

21 To be legal, third party insurance must cover: (2)

a Injury to another person.

b Injury to yourself.

c Damage to someone's property.

d Damage to your vehicle.

22 You must produce your motor insurance certificate: (2)

a When requested to do so by a police officer.

b When selling your motor vehicle.

c At a motorway toll booth.

d When taxing your vehicle.

23 The cost of vehicle insurance may be reduced if: (2)

a You are older than 21.

b You are older than 25.

c You have passed GCSEs.

d You complete a Pass Plus training scheme.

24 Which of the following statements are correct? (2)

a A motor car must have an MOT certificate once it is three years old.

b An MOT certificate is valid for three years.

c An MOT certificate is valid for one year.

d A caravan requires an MOT certificate every two years.

YOU AND YOUR VEHICLE

| 24 a, c | 23 b, d | 22 a, d | 21 a, c | 20 c, d | 19 a, b |
| 18 c | 17 a | 16 c, d | 15 c | 14 a, b | 13 b, c |

21

5 Vehicle and passenger safety and security

The safety and security of vehicle and passengers are the responsibility of the driver. There are certain measures that can be taken to protect the security of the vehicle and the safety of passengers, and regular checking and maintenance will ensure that the vehicle is in good working order. Your vehicle must comply with the requirements of the Road Vehicles Regulations (Constructions and Use).

 ## Vehicle safety checks

Before the Practical Driving Test begins the examiner will ask you a series of 'show and tell' questions about checking your vehicle for safety. For cars and motorcycles, one or two wrong answers in each section will result in one 'driving fault' being recorded. For a car with trailer, each wrong answer will result in a 'driving fault' being recorded, up to a maximum of four driving faults. If you answer more than four questions incorrectly a 'serious fault' will result.

Show

▶ Show where you would check the following items:
- engine oil level (car & m/cycle);
- engine coolant level (car);
- windscreen washer reservoir (car);
- brake fluid reservoir (car & m/cycle).

▶ Show how you would check that the following items are working / in good condition:
- headlights (car & m/cycle);
- tail lights (car & m/cycle);
- direction indicators (car);
- horn (car & m/cycle) (off-road only);
- power steering before a journey (car).

For motorcycles, show also where you would check:
- emergency engine stop switch;
- brakes;
- steering for excessive play;
- lights, brake lights and reflectors . . .

For a car with trailer, show also:
- how to check that the vehicle and trailer doors are secure . . .

Tell

▶ Tell how you would check that:
- the engine has enough oil (car & m/cycle);
- the engine has the correct coolant level (car);
- the windscreen washer reservoir has enough water in it (car);
- there is a safe level of hydraulic brake fluid in the reservoir (car & m/cycle);
- the brake lights are working (car & m/cycle);
- the brakes are working before starting a journey (car & m/cycle);
- the tyre tread is deep enough (car & m/cycle);
- the general condition of the tyres is safe for use on the road (car & m/cycle);
- the power-assisted steering is working before the journey (car).

. . . and tell:
- how you would check the condition of the chain.

. . . and explain:
- the main safety factors for loading;
- how to secure a load safely.

Tyres

▌ Tyre pressures must be checked when the tyres are cold.

▌ Check your tyre pressures weekly and before a journey.

▌ Under-inflated tyres can cause heavy steering, poor braking and increased fuel consumption.

▌ Tyres should be inflated above normal pressure when:
  – driving fast;
  – travelling for a long distance;
  – carrying a heavy load.

▌ Tyres must not have large deep cuts in the sidewalls.

▌ Tyres must have a minimum tread depth over the central three-quarters of the breadth of the tyre, around the entire circumference, as follows:
  – cars, light vans and light trailers: **1.6 mm**

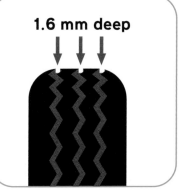

1.6 mm deep

  – motorcycles, large vehicles and passenger-carrying vehicles: **1.0 mm**
  – mopeds: **a visible tread**

▌ Worn tyres increase the stopping distance.

▌ Uneven tyre wear can be caused by faults in the braking system, the suspension or the wheel alignment.

 Tyres

▌ Remember, vehicles with defective tyres are not suitable for the test.

Lights

Make sure that your vehicle complies fully with the requirements of the Road Vehicles Lighting Regulations.

▌ Lights, indicators, reflectors and number plates must be kept clear of dirt.

▌ Lights must be correctly adjusted to avoid dazzling other road users, especially if the vehicle is heavily loaded.

 Lights

▌ Remember, vehicles with defective lights are not suitable for the test.

Maintenance

▌ The following must be in good working order for the vehicle to be roadworthy:
  – speedometer;
  – windscreen washer;
  – windscreen wipers;
  – horn.

▌ The following must be kept in good condition:
  – headlights;
  – windscreen;
  – seatbelts.

▌ Before making a long motorway journey, check your vehicle because continuous high speed increases the risk of a breakdown.

▌ Before a long journey, check:
  – the oil level, and add oil if necessary;
  – that you have enough fuel for the journey;
  – the radiator coolant level;
  – tyre pressures and condition.

▌ If the engine has overheated, wait for the engine to cool normally before adding coolant or water to the radiator.

YOU AND YOUR VEHICLE

- Check your brake fluid weekly because low brake fluid can cause an accident.
- Have the battery checked before winter, and check the battery-water level regularly.
- To check the shock absorbers, press down on a corner of the vehicle, and then release it. If the vehicle continues to bounce repeatedly, this indicates that the shock absorbers might be worn.
- Fuel can be wasted by:
  – carrying unnecessary weight;
  – an empty roof rack;
  – under-inflated tyres;
  – a loose fuel cap;
  – heavy accelerating and braking.
- Driving at 70 mph can use up to 30% more fuel than driving at 50 mph.
- After refuelling, ensure that the fuel cap is secure to prevent leaking fuel, which makes the road slippery for other road users.

Seatbelts

- Wear a seatbelt unless you are exempt.
- Those exempt include:
  – holders of a medical exemption certificate;
  – people making local deliveries in a custom-designed delivery vehicle.
- You may remove your seatbelt while reversing.
- Ensure that children under 14 years of age either wear a seatbelt or have an approved child restraint, such as:
  – a child seat;
  – a harness;
  – a baby carrier.
- You must wear a seatbelt in a minibus with an unladen weight of 2,540 kg or less.
- In larger minibuses and coaches you should wear a seatbelt if one is fitted.

Seatbelts

- The examiner will be watching your use of the seatbelt.

Children in vehicles

- Do not allow children to sit behind the rear seat of an estate car or hatchback unless in a specially fitted child seat.
- When carrying children, activate the child safety locks on the rear doors, if fitted.
- Keep children under control.
- Never fit a rear-facing baby seat on a seat protected by an airbag.

- Don't leave children or pets in an unventilated vehicle.

Requirements for seatbelts

A tick indicates which seats require seatbelts to be worn.

	Front seat	Rear seat	Responsibility
Driver	✔		Driver
Child under 3	✔ (restraint)	✔ (restraint if available)	Driver
Child 3–11 or <1.5 m tall	✔ restraint or adult seatbelt	✔ restraint or adult seatbelt if available	Driver
Child 12–13 or >1.5 m tall	✔	✔ seatbelt if available	Driver
Passenger over 14	✔	✔ seatbelt if available	Passenger

Emergency measures

▶ You should have the following items in your vehicle:
– fire extinguisher;
– first aid kit;
– warning triangle.

▶ Whenever there is a strong smell of petrol, check it out.

▶ If the vehicle catches fire:
– get all occupants out and away from the vehicle;
– don't open the bonnet to extinguish a blaze;
– call the fire brigade.

Anti-theft measures

▶ When leaving your vehicle:
– take all valuables with you, or lock them out of sight;
– lock all the windows and doors.

▶ Have your vehicle registration number etched on all the vehicle windows

▶ If possible, install a security-coded radio.

▶ Don't leave the vehicle documents inside the vehicle.

▶ If possible, install an immobilizer.

▶ If possible, park in a secure car park or well-lit area at night to reduce the risk of a break-in.

▶ Inside a garage is the safest place to park a vehicle.

▶ When parking and leaving your vehicle, engage the steering lock.

▶ Lock your vehicle and remove the key when leaving your vehicle parked and unattended.

▶ Display vehicle-watch stickers in the windscreen to invite the police to stop your vehicle if it is seen in use during certain times.

Pollution control

▶ Motor vehicles can harm the environment in terms of:
– air pollution;
– damage to buildings;
– using up natural resources.

▶ Trams are environmentally friendly because they:
– reduce noise pollution;
– use electricity;
– reduce town traffic.

▶ MOT tests include a strict emission test to help protect the environment against pollution.

▶ Modern vehicles have catalytic converters on the exhaust system to reduce exhaust emissions.

▶ Have your vehicle serviced regularly to keep exhaust emissions cleaner and give better fuel economy.

▶ You can help the environment by:
– reducing speed;
– accelerating gently rather than harshly;
– using low-sulphur unleaded petrol;

– having your vehicle serviced properly;
– using correct tyre pressures;
– not over-revving in lower gears;
– watching the traffic and planning ahead;
– not making a lot of short journeys;
– using public transport more often;
– sharing a car when possible;

– walking or cycling for short journeys;
– disposing of old oil at an authorized site;
– disposing of a used battery at a local authority site, or taking it to a garage.

Pollution control

The vehicle should not be smoking excessively or have a noisy exhaust.

Vehicle and passenger safety and security

The number in brackets at the end of each question indicates how many correct answers you should mark.

1 Which of the following apply? (2)

a Tyres should be inflated above normal pressure when driving short distances.

b Under-inflated tyres can cause heavy steering.

c Under-inflated tyres reduce fuel consumption.

d Tyres should be inflated above normal pressure when driving fast.

2 What is the minimum required tread depth for motor-car tyres? (1)

a 1.6 mm.

b 2.0 mm.

c 2.5 mm.

d 1.9 mm.

3 Which of the following are correct? (2)

a Mopeds must have a visible tread pattern.

b Heavy vehicles must have a minimum of 1 mm tread depth

c Heavy vehicles must have a minimum tread depth of 2 mm.

d Mopeds must have a minimum of 1 mm tread depth across 80% of the tread width.

4 Under what conditions is the stopping distance increased? (1)

a When you are travelling slowly.

b When the tyres are brand new.

c When you brake sharply.

d When the tyres are worn.

5 Which of the following must be in good working order for a vehicle to be roadworthy? (2)

a Seat covers.

b Steering wheel lock.

c Windscreen wipers.

d Windscreen washers.

6 What must be checked before going on a long journey? (1)

a The coolant level.

b The condition of the silencer.

c The air conditioning gases.

d The operation of the heater.

7 Which of the following can waste fuel? (2)

a An empty roof rack.

b A loose fuel cap.

c Driving with the windows open.

d Driving too slowly.

8 In respect of seatbelts, which of the following statements is true? (1)

a The elderly are exempt from wearing seatbelts.

b Children under the age of 16 don't need seatbelts.

c You can remove the seatbelt when reversing.

d Use of seatbelts in the back seats is not necessary.

9 Which of the following items should be kept in the vehicle in case of an emergency? (1)

a Fire extinguisher.

b A mobile phone.

c A puncture repair kit.

d Moist towels.

10 Which of the following are anti-theft measures? (3)

a Parking in a well-illuminated area at night.

b Etching the vehicle registration number on all the windows.

c Installing an immobilizer.

d Keeping a warning triangle visible inside the vehicle.

11 In which way can motor vehicles harm the environment? (1)

a Water pollution.

b Noise pollution.

c Air pollution.

d Oxidizing paint.

12 Why do modern vehicles have catalytic converters? (1)

a To cool the radiator more efficiently.

b To improve engine lubrication.

c To reduce exhaust noise.

d To reduce exhaust emissions.

1 b, d	2 a	3 a, b	4 d	5 c, d	6 a
7 a, b	8 c	9 a	10 a, b, c	11 c	12 d

Vehicle control

The lives of other road users, your passengers and yourself depend on the manner in which you handle your vehicle and use the various controls.

Vehicle control

You must demonstrate that you know and understand the functions of all the various controls. They must be used smoothly, correctly, safely, at the correct time, and competently. You must also be able to perform various routine safety checks and identify defects.

Things you must do

▶ Know the functions of, and where to find, the following controls:
  – indicators;
  – lights;
  – windscreen wipers;
  – demisters;
  – heater.
▶ Understand the meaning of the various gauges and lights on the instrument panel.
▶ Know how to check the levels of the oil and the coolant.
▶ Know how to identify defects in
  – steering;
  – brakes;
  – tyres;
  – seatbelts;
  – lights;

  – reflectors;
  – horn;
  – rear view mirrors;
  – speedometer;
  – exhaust system;
  – direction indicators;
  – windscreen wipers and washers.

Accelerator and clutch

▶ The 'kick-down' feature on an automatic transmission enables the driver to change to a lower gear for faster acceleration.

Accelerator and clutch

You must demonstrate that you can use the accelerator and clutch smoothly, correctly and safely.

Things you must do
▶ Balance the use of the clutch and accelerator to pull away smoothly.

▶ In an automatic vehicle, depress the brake pedal when you engage 'Drive'.
▶ Accelerate gradually to increase speed.
▶ In a manual vehicle, depress the clutch pedal just before the car stops.

Some don'ts
▶ Don't accelerate too harshly and make the wheels spin and screech.
▶ Don't use the clutch in a manner that makes the vehicle jerk when moving off.

Use of mirrors

▶ Look in the mirrors before:
  – signalling;
  – stopping;
  – moving off;
  – changing direction;
  – changing lane;
  – changing speed;
  – opening your door.

▶ Remember to use the Mirrors – Signal – Manoeuvre (M-S-M) routine.

▶ Check in the mirrors:
  – frequently to see what is happening behind and alongside your vehicle;
  – in good time before changing speed or direction, and before signalling;
  – before slowing down or stopping.

▶ Look over your shoulder to check what is happening in the blind spots (the areas not seen in the mirrors) before moving off, or changing direction or lane.

▶ Curved mirrors give a wider field of vision, but do not eliminate blind spots.

▶ When towing a caravan, fit extended-arm side mirrors to get a better view behind and around you.

Use of mirrors

The examiner will be checking that you use the mirrors correctly when you drive, including use of the Mirrors – Signal – Manoeuvre (M-S-M) routine.

▶ *Mirrors*
Before signalling, check the position of traffic and any pedestrians around and behind you.

▶ *Signal*
Indicate in good time your intention to slow down, change course or stop.

▶ *Manoeuvre*
If safe to do so, execute the intended manoeuvre (e.g. changing speed or direction).

Braking and gears

▶ To avoid locking the wheels when stopping, apply the brakes early and lightly, and then with more pressure.

▶ To avoid stopping with a jolt, release the pressure as the vehicle comes to a stop.

▶ Don't brake harshly except in an emergency.

▶ In an emergency, apply the brakes immediately and avoid locking the wheels to prevent skidding.

▶ If the vehicle does skid, release the brake pressure and steer in the direction to which the back of the vehicle is skidding.

▶ After driving through deep water or flooding, test the brakes gently.

▶ Wet brakes are not effective, so brake lightly while driving slowly to dry them off.

▶ If the vehicle pulls to one side, have the brakes checked at a garage.

▶ Excessive use of brakes can cause overheating and brake failure. Use a lower gear to assist braking when going downhill.

▶ If the brake warning light comes on, have the brakes checked immediately.

▶ Anti-lock brakes prevent wheels from locking so that tyres are less likely to skid and steering control is easier.

▶ Anti-lock brakes may not always prevent skidding on wet surfaces, dry gravel or shingle surfaces.

▶ Anti-lock brakes are most effective when you brake suddenly and excessively. (They start to work just as the wheels are about to lock.)

▶ You can steer a vehicle with anti-lock brakes while you are braking.

Braking and gears

You must demonstrate that you can use the footbrake and gears smoothly and progressively.

Things you must do

▷ Depress the footbrake smoothly and in good time so as not to lock the wheels.

▷ Brake lightly at first, then apply more pressure to bring the vehicle to a stop.

▷ Select and use the correct gear for your speed and circumstances.

▷ Change gear in good time to avoid labouring the engine.

▷ If necessary, select a lower gear to control the vehicle speed near a hazard.

▷ Apply the handbrake to hold the vehicle when queuing or whenever the vehicle will be stationary for a period of time.

Some don'ts

▷ Don't brake harshly, except in an emergency.

▷ Don't apply the handbrake while the vehicle is still moving.

▷ Don't move off with the handbrake still on.

▷ Don't take your eyes off the road when changing gear.

▷ Don't coast with the clutch pedal depressed or with the gear lever in neutral.

Steering

▷ Except when changing gears, keep both hands on the steering wheel in the ten-to-two or quarter-to-three position, to maintain full control of the vehicle.

▷ Under-inflated front tyres will cause the steering to feel heavy.

▷ Turning the steering wheel while the car is stationary will damage both the steering and the tyres.

Steering

You must demonstrate your ability to steer the vehicle on a proper course without creating a dangerous situation.

Things you must do

▷ Steer with steady, smooth movements.

▷ Begin turning the steering wheel at the correct time when turning around a corner.

Some don'ts

▷ Don't allow the steering wheel to spin back after turning.

▷ Don't rest your arm on the door.

▷ When turning right, don't turn too soon and cut the corner.

▷ Don't bump or mount the kerb when turning left.

▷ Don't turn too wide or too late.

▷ Don't cross your hands on the wheel when turning.

Coasting

▷ When coasting (moving in neutral or with the clutch depressed):
  – the engine has no braking power;
  – speed downhill increases rapidly;

  – the effectiveness of the footbrake is reduced;
  – there is reduced steering control on curves;
  – gear selection may be difficult.

Coasting

The examiner will be watching to see if you run on in neutral, or with the clutch pedal depressed.

▷ Don't coast with the clutch pedal depressed or with the gear lever in neutral.

Vehicle control

The number in brackets at the end of each question indicates how many correct answers you should mark.

1 What does the automatic transmission kick-down feature enable the driver to do? (1)

a Adjust the vehicle's speed.

b Change up to a higher gear to reduce the engine revolutions.

c Slow down in an emergency.

d Change down to a lower gear for faster acceleration.

2 When should you look in the mirrors? (2)

a Before signalling.

b After changing lane, speed or direction.

c Before opening your door.

d After stopping.

3 What is the M-S-M procedure? (1)

a Move, Stop, Manoeuvre.

b Mirrors, Signal, Manoeuvre.

c Move, Stop, Move again.

d Manoeuvre, Signal, Move off.

4 Why should you look in the mirrors frequently? (1)

a To monitor traffic flow behind you.

b To see what is happening around your vehicle.

c To see how far ahead you are of the vehicle behind you.

d To see how many vehicles are behind you.

5 How do you see what is happening in the blind spots? (1)

a Switch the headlights on.

b Use the external mirrors.

c Look over your shoulder.

d Switch on the interior light.

6 When should you look in the blind spots? (2)

a When driving in the dark.

b Before moving off.

c Before changing lane or direction.

d When the mirrors are broken.

7 Which statements are true about curved mirrors? (2)

a They bring the images closer.

b They give a wider field of vision.

c They eliminate the blind spots.

d They do not eliminate the blind spots.

8 For a better view behind you when towing a caravan you should: (1)

a Keep the caravan's curtains open.

b Fit an extended-arm mirror on the driver's side.

c Fit an extended-arm mirror on the passenger's side.

d Fit extended-arm mirrors on both sides.

9 How can you avoid locking the wheels when stopping? (1)

a Use the gears instead of the brakes.

b First use the gears to slow the vehicle down, then use the brakes.

c Apply the brakes early and heavily, then more lightly.

d Apply the brakes early and lightly, then with more pressure.

10 How do you avoid stopping with a jolt? (1)

a Use the handbrake to slow the vehicle down smoothly.

b Release the brake pressure as the vehicle comes to a stop.

c Use the handbrake for the last part of the stopping only.

d Slow down extremely gradually before stopping.

11 Under what circumstance can you brake harshly? (1)

a To test your brakes.

b In an emergency.

c When there are children crossing the road.

d In rainy weather.

12 What effect will under-inflated tyres have? (1)

a The ride will be smoother.

b Steering will be easier.

c The steering will feel light.

d Steering will feel heavy.

7 b, d	8 d	9 d	10 b	11 b	12 d
1 d	2 a, c	3 b	4 b	5 c	6 b, c

Speed control

▶ Don't drive faster than the maximum speed limit for the road, and for your class of vehicle.

▶ Reduce speed when:
 – the road layout or condition is hazardous;
 – approaching a junction;
 – there are pedestrians, children, cyclists or motorcyclists on the road;

 – bad weather conditions prevail;
 – driving at night or in poor visibility;
 – you wish to reduce fuel consumption.

▶ Harsh braking and accelerating will increase fuel consumption.

▶ Select a lower gear to help control your speed, especially going downhill.

▶ Select the correct gear for the speed and circumstances.

▶ Change gear in good time and don't labour the engine.

▶ Don't take your eyes off the road when changing gear.

▶ When going uphill, vehicles slow down and their engines work harder.

 ## Speed control

You must be able to drive at a speed that is appropriate for the traffic, road conditions and weather, and that is in accordance with any road signs and speed limits. The examiner will be watching how carefully you control your speed as you drive.

Things you must do

▶ Drive at a safe speed and comply with all speed limits.

▶ Maintain a safe following distance behind the vehicle ahead of you.

▶ Increase the following distance on wet or slippery roads.

Some don'ts

▶ Don't drive too fast or too slowly for the traffic conditions.

▶ Don't change speed unpredictably.

Making progress

You will be expected to make reasonable progress along a road by driving at an appropriate speed, and to move off at junctions as soon as it is safe to do so. The examiner will be watching your confidence, judgement, and response to the traffic, road and weather conditions.

Things you must do

▶ Make progress by driving at a realistic speed.

▶ Keep up with the traffic around you.

▶ Show confidence and sound judgement.

▶ Drive in accordance with the road traffic signs and speed limits.

▶ Adjust your speed according to the type of road, the traffic, the weather and visibility.

Some don'ts

▶ Don't hold up the traffic by driving too slowly.

▶ Don't wait too long when it is safe to move off.

▶ Don't hold up traffic by reducing speed too soon when you approach a junction.

Stopping and following distances

▶ Maintain a safe following distance so that you can pull up safely if the vehicle in front of you slows down or stops suddenly.

▶ Don't follow too closely (known as 'tailgating').

▶ Adjust your speed according to the road, traffic and weather conditions. (Speed limits are the maximum speed allowable, and not necessarily the safe speed for particular driving or weather conditions.)

▶ In good conditions, on roads carrying fast traffic, maintain at least a two-second gap behind the vehicle in front of you.

▶ On wet roads double the following distance, and in icy conditions increase it by ten times.

▶ Large vehicles, vehicles carrying loads and motorcycles require a longer stopping distance.

In slow-moving traffic:

▶ Maintain a following distance between you and the vehicle in front of you that will enable you to stop safely.

▶ To maintain smooth traffic flow, reduce the following distance.

▶ Maintain sufficient space to manoeuvre if the vehicle ahead breaks down, or to allow an emergency vehicle through.

🚗 Stopping and following distances

Following other vehicles

The examiner will be watching to see that you can stop safely within the distance you can see to be clear ahead.

Things you must do

▶ Maintain a safe following distance behind the vehicle ahead of you.

▶ Vary the gap according to the weather and changing road and traffic conditions.

▶ Use the M-S-M routine.

▶ Reduce speed if you need to.

▶ Look out for brake lights and indicators on vehicles ahead of you.

▶ Anticipate situations that could develop.

▶ Use the controls appropriately.

Some don'ts

▶ Don't follow any vehicle too closely.

▶ Don't brake suddenly.

▶ Don't stop too close to a vehicle ahead of you.

Typical stopping distances

■ Thinking distance
■ Braking distance

average car length = 4 metres

20 mph		= 12 metres (40 feet) or 3 car lengths
	6 6	
30 mph		= 23 metres (75 feet) or 6 car lengths
	9 14	
40 mph		= 36 metres (120 feet) or 9 car lengths
	12 24	
50 mph		= 53 metres (175 feet) or 13 car lengths
	15 38	
60 mph		= 73 metres (240 feet) or 18 car lengths
	18 55	
70 mph		= 96 metres (315 feet) or 24 car lengths
	21 75	

Towing

- Passengers may not ride in a caravan being towed.

- Don't tow more than your licence allows.
- Don't exceed the manufacturer's recommended towing weight for your vehicle.
- To avoid losing control of the trailer or caravan:
  - distribute the weight evenly, with heavy items above the axle;
  - ensure that there is downward pressure on the tow hitch;
  - don't exceed the manufacturer's recommended weight for the tow hitch.
- When towing a caravan, a stabilizer fitted to the towbar will improve vehicle handling.
- A breakaway cable is an additional safety device that can be fitted to a trailer braking system.
- If the trailer or caravan starts to swerve or 'snake', reduce speed gently without braking.
- Allow extra space for overtaking and manoeuvring.
- Allow longer space for braking (because of extra weight).
- Allow for slower acceleration (because of extra weight).

Towing

Towing a trailer

You must have a full category B driving licence before towing a trailer or caravan up to 750 kg, provided that the vehicle and trailer together do not exceed 3.5 tonnes. If you wish to tow a heavier trailer, you must first pass a Practical Category B+E Test.

When you practise driving with a trailer you must display L- or D-plates, front and rear, and you must be accompanied by a person who has held a category B+E licence for at least three years and is 21 years or older. You should practise on different types of roads in different traffic conditions. You must practise reversing, turning left and right, and uncoupling and recoupling the trailer.

The same vehicle requirements apply as for the vehicle of any new driver, and the trailer must also be roadworthy. If the vehicle or trailer don't meet the requirements, the test will be cancelled and you will lose your fee.

Eyesight test

The test includes the same eyesight test as for a new driver. See page 15 for details.

Reversing

You must reverse the trailer into a restricted space on the offside of your vehicle:

- under good control and in a reasonable time;
- making good observations;
- with reasonable accuracy;
- inside a clearly defined boundary;

so that the rear of the trailer ends up within a yellow painted box area in the bay.

Things you must do
- Reverse under full control.
- Use good all-round observation.
- Judge the size of your vehicle accurately.

Some don'ts
- Don't approach the starting point too fast or at an angle.
- Don't stop beyond the first markers.
- Don't turn the steering wheel incorrectly when starting to reverse.
- Don't allow any wheels to cross the yellow boundary lines.
- Don't move off without following the M-S-M routine.
- Don't touch any of the cones or markers.
- Don't stop short of or beyond the yellow painted box area.

Braking

You will be required to travel at about 20 mph and then execute a controlled stop after passing two markers.

Things you must do
- Stop under full control.
- Stop as quickly as possible.
- Stop as safely as possible.
- Stop in a straight line.

Some don'ts
- Don't travel below 20 mph.
- Don't brake too soon.
- Don't cause a skid.
- Don't stall the engine.
- Don't take too long to stop.

The drive

You will be required to drive on a variety of roads and to demonstrate that you can move off safely on the level, uphill, downhill, normally from the side of a road, and at an angle. You won't be required to reverse around a corner, make an emergency stop, reverse park or turn in the road.

You must demonstrate that you can safely do the following things:

▶ Meet other vehicles.

▶ Overtake.

▶ Cross the path of other vehicles.

▶ Keep an appropriate following distance.

▶ Negotiate roundabouts.

Other things you must do

▶ Exercise correct lane discipline.

▶ Display courtesy and consideration to other road users.

▶ Apply the correct procedure at pedestrian crossings, level crossings, junctions and traffic signals.

▶ Use the mirrors effectively.

▶ Use signals correctly.

▶ Stay alert and anticipate the actions of other road users.

▶ Use speed correctly.

▶ Observe the speed limits.

▶ Use the vehicle controls correctly.

What you must not do

▶ Don't negotiate hazards and junctions dangerously.

Uncoupling a trailer

You will be asked to park where it is safe on a level stretch of ground and demonstrate uncoupling.

Things you must do

▶ Ensure that the handbrakes of the vehicle and the trailer are both applied.

▶ Set the anti-reverse mechanism where applicable.

▶ Lower the jockey wheel on to the ground.

▶ Disconnect the electric cable and stow it out of the way.

▶ Remove any stabilizer equipment.

▶ Remove any safety chain or link.

▶ Release the coupling and lift the trailer off the towbar using the jockey wheel.

▶ Move the vehicle forward about one vehicle length.

Recoupling a trailer

You will be asked to reverse the vehicle and to couple up the trailer.

Things you must do

▶ Reverse the vehicle to a position where the trailer can be easily coupled, and apply the parking brake.

▶ Attach the trailer to the vehicle's towbar.

▶ Secure any safety chain or device.

▶ If necessary, install any stabilizing equipment.

▶ Connect the electric cable.

▶ Make sure that the coupling is secure.

▶ If necessary, raise any lifting legs or jockey wheel.

▶ Make sure that the vehicle handbrake is on, and only then release the trailer brake.

▶ Check the operation of the trailer lights and indicators.

Some don'ts

▶ Don't move off without raising the lifting legs or jockey wheel.

▶ Don't move off without first checking the:

– lights;

– indicators;

– safety chain;

– trailer handbrake is released.

Loads on and in vehicles

 ### Loads on and in vehicles

You must be able to explain the effect on a vehicle's performance of a loaded roof rack and luggage as well as extra passengers.

▶ Luggage must always be securely and safely stowed.

▶ The driver is responsible for ensuring that the vehicle is not overloaded.

▶ Steering and vehicle handling can be adversely affected by a loaded roof rack, extra passengers and overloading.

▶ Don't overload your vehicle or trailer.

▶ Don't exceed the vehicle manufacturer's recommended tow weight.

- The load must be securely fastened to the vehicle.
- The load must not stick out dangerously.
- A heavy load on a roof rack will reduce vehicle stability.

Emergency stopping

- To reduce the chance of skidding when stopping quickly with anti-lock brakes, brake rapidly and firmly, without releasing the brake pedal until you have stopped.
- In the event of a burst tyre:
  - hold the steering wheel firmly;
  - pull up slowly to the side of the road (without using the brakes if it is a front tyre).

Emergency stopping

You may be required to perform an emergency stop. The examiner will direct you to stop on the side of the road and ask you to perform an emergency stop when signalled to do so. The signal to stop will be demonstrated to you. You will then be asked to move off again and to perform the emergency stop when the signal is given. On that signal, you must stop as quickly as possible, without locking the wheels, keeping the vehicle safely under control.

Things you must do

- Be prepared for the signal, which could come at any time.
- React as quickly as possible by applying the footbrake.
- Bring the vehicle to a controlled stop as quickly as possible.
- Stop in a straight line.
- Take extra care in wet or slippery conditions.

Some don'ts

- Don't stop before you are signalled to do so.
- Don't lose control of the vehicle.
- Don't create a dangerous situation for other traffic.

Headlights and sidelights

- Switch on the headlights while driving at night, except on 'restricted roads'. (These are roads with streetlights not more than 185 metres apart and usually with a speed limit of 30 mph.)
- Switch on the headlights when visibility is restricted to 100 metres (328 ft), and at dusk, even if streetlights are not lit, so that others can see you.
- Sidelights and rear registration plate lights must be switched on at night.
- Don't dazzle other road users or cause them discomfort with your vehicle lights:
  - Dip the headlights for oncoming traffic and when following closely behind another vehicle.

- Apply the handbrake rather than the footbrake when queuing at night, to avoid dazzling the driver behind with your stop light.
- When overtaking, keep the headlights dipped until you are alongside the other vehicle, and only then switch to the main beam, if necessary.
- When being overtaken, dip your headlights as soon as the vehicle passes you.

- If you are dazzled by oncoming headlights, slow down and stop if necessary.
- If you are dazzled by the headlights of the vehicle behind you, set your rear view mirror to anti-dazzle.
- At night in built-up areas, and also in dull daytime weather, use dipped headlights so that you are easily seen by others.

YOU AND YOUR VEHICLE

- In a dangerous situation, flash your headlights to warn other road users of your presence.
- Don't flash your headlights to intimidate road users, to greet others, to show impatience or to give up your priority.
- When stationary, don't proceed because another motorist has flashed the headlights; use your own judgement.

Fog lights

- In good visibility fog lights can dazzle other drivers.
- Rear fog lights can appear to be brake lights and should not be used when visibility is good.

- Use front and rear fog lights only when visibility is seriously reduced to less than 100 metres (328 ft).
- Switch off any fog lights when visibility improves.

Hazard warning lights

- Use hazard warning lights:
  – to warn other motorists that your vehicle is stationary and a temporary obstruction;
  – on a motorway or an unrestricted dual carriageway only if you need to warn drivers behind you of a hazard or obstruction ahead.

- Don't use hazard warning lights:
  – for longer than necessary;
  – in any other situation while moving;
  – as an excuse for dangerous or illegal parking.

The horn

- Don't sound your horn:
  – while stationary;
  – while driving in a built-up area between 11.30 pm and 7.00 am (flash your headlights instead);
  – for reasons of aggression.

- Sound your horn only:
  – when another vehicle poses a danger; or
  – when moving and you need to alert other motorists to your presence.

YOU AND YOUR VEHICLE

Reversing

▶ Don't reverse into a main road from a side road.

▶ Don't reverse or turn around in a busy road; use a quiet road.
▶ Before reversing, check in all the mirrors to ensure that it is safe to reverse.
▶ Check in the blind spots just before moving.
▶ Look out for pedestrians, children, cyclists or obstructions behind you.
▶ Look mainly through the rear window when reversing.

EYE 1234

▶ When reversing and turning, make sure it is safe all around you, because the front of the vehicle will swing out to the side as it turns.
▶ If necessary, ask someone to guide you, or get out of your vehicle and check yourself.

▶ Don't reverse further than necessary.
▶ On driveways, if possible reverse in and drive out forwards.

Reversing

Reversing around a corner

You will be instructed to stop on the side of the road and the examiner will explain this manoeuvre to you. You will be required to reverse around a corner while maintaining full control of the vehicle, without bumping or mounting the kerb, and while performing effective all-round observations. You can remove your seatbelt for this part of the test.

Things you must do

▶ Look in the mirrors and blind spots before moving off, to ensure that it is safe to do so.
▶ Signal your intention to turn.
▶ Begin to reverse around the corner when it is safe to do so, while keeping a lookout for pedestrians and other traffic.
▶ Straighten up as the vehicle completes the turn and reverse in a straight line for a reasonable distance.
▶ Stop and wait for the examiner's next instruction.
▶ Make sure that the indicator has cancelled.

Some don'ts

▶ Don't mount or bump the kerb.
▶ Don't swing out too far from the kerb.
▶ Don't be inconsiderate towards other road users.
▶ Don't take too long to complete the manoeuvre.
▶ Don't turn the steering wheel when the vehicle is stationary.

Vehicle control continued

The number in brackets at the end of each question indicates how many correct answers you should mark.

13 When may you remove one hand from the steering wheel? (1)

a When the road is smooth and straight.

b When switching on the lights.

c When changing gears.

d When waving to other motorists.

14 What three risks occur during coasting? (3)

a The engine has no braking power.

b Fuel consumption is less.

c Speed downhill increases rapidly.

d The footbrake is less effective.

15 What two risks occur during coasting? (2)

a Steering control is more difficult on curves.

b Fuel consumption increases.

c The vehicle may backfire.

d Gear selection may be difficult.

16 Which situations call for a reduction in speed? (3)

a Where there is a junction ahead.

b Pedestrians, children, cyclists or motorcyclists on the road.

c Bad weather.

d Bright sunlight.

17 How can you help to control speed downhill? (1)

a Brake harshly.

b Apply the handbrake.

c Change down to a lower gear.

d Apply the footbrake and handbrake together.

18 What should you *not* do when changing gears? (1)

a Skip a gear.

b Wiggle the gear lever.

c Depress the clutch.

d Take your eyes off the road.

19 What gap should you keep between you and the vehicle ahead of you in good conditions? (1)

a At least 20 metres.

b At least 1 second.

c At least 2 seconds.

d At least 10 metres.

20 By how much should you increase the following distance during icy conditions? (1)

a Twice.

b By ten times.

c By five times.

d By four times.

21 How can you reduce the chance of skidding with anti-lock brakes? (2)

a Brake lightly at first, then more firmly until you have stopped.

b Brake harshly at first, then more lightly until you have stopped.

c Brake rapidly and firmly.

d Keep the pedal depressed until you have stopped.

22 When should the headlights be switched on? (3)

a When driving at night.

b When visibility is restricted to 100 metres.

c At dusk.

d While driving on 'restricted' roads.

23 Which two statements are wrong? (2)

a Fog lights should not be used when visibility is good.

b Hazard warning lights may never be used when moving.

c You may reverse into a main road from a side road.

d If you are dazzled by oncoming headlights, slow down and stop if necessary.

24 Which three statements are correct for reversing? (3)

a Use mainly the rear view mirrors.

b If necessary, ask someone to guide you, or get out of the vehicle and check yourself.

c Check in the blind spots just before moving.

d Look mainly through the rear window.

13	c	14	a, c, d	15	a, d	16	a, b, c	17	c	18	d
19	c	20	b	21	c, d	22	a, b, c	23	b, c	24	b, c, d

7 The road signage system

There are essentially three kinds of message conveyed by road signs, and each has a basic shape to help the road user identify what kind of message it contains. Signs and signals specific to motorways are explained in Chapter 15 (see pages 104–10).

Circular signs give orders.

Triangular signs warn.

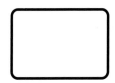

Rectangular signs inform.

The colour combinations used with these three basic shapes give additional information about what the signs mean.

- A blue circular sign with a thin white border gives orders – it tells what the road user *must* do.

- A white circular sign with a wide red border prohibits – it tells what is *not allowed*.

- Blue rectangular signs on general roads give useful information.

- On motorways they indicate directions.

- Green horizontal rectangular signs indicate directions on primary routes.

- White horizontal rectangular signs with a black border indicate directions on non-primary routes.

- They are also used as supplementary plates to go with other signs, such as warning signs and regulatory signs.

- Brown rectangular signs help to direct drivers to tourist attractions and facilities.

- Other shapes and colour combinations may be used to give prominence to certain signs.

Road signs are often supported by road markings painted on the surface of the carriageway.

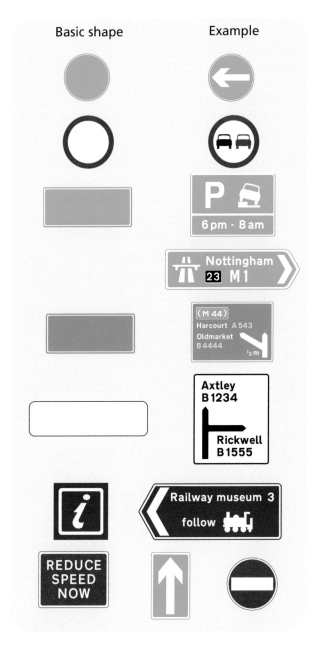

Basic shape   Example

The road signs learn-and-test system

The information you need to know about road signs is given in groups of signs, and in two study formats.

First, there is introductory information with a selection of signs to learn. You must know these signs and their meanings. Where an asterisk (*) appears with the sign name or description, this means that there could be both left and right versions of the sign, and in some cases a straight-ahead version too.

Second, each section of road signs and information is followed by an illustrated learn-and-test section for that group of signs. In these sections, for each road sign given, you should first read the information in the left-hand column and study the picture in the middle column. Make sure you understand the meaning and context of each sign. Ignore the right-hand column while studying. Study a whole page in this way and then cover up the first two columns to answer the test-yourself questions in the right-hand column, without looking at the correct answers given at the bottom of the page. This means: learn a page, test the page.

For some questions you must select only one of the options listed. In other questions you must select two or more, as specified. So read the instructions carefully.

Once you have answered all the questions on that page, check your answers by referring to the bottom of the page. If you have selected an incorrect answer, study the information and the picture again and make sure that you understand why your selection was wrong. Mark the page and test yourself on it again later.

8 Warning signs

Warning signs indicate potentially hazardous conditions ahead. Generally, warning signs are a red triangle on a white background, although there are some exceptions.

General response to all warning signs

▶ Approach with caution and slow down if necessary.

▶ Take note of any other road signs and obey any regulatory signs or signals.

▶ Anticipate any possible hazard according to the nature of the warning, for example:
- children or animals running on to the road;
- other vulnerable road users such as pedestrians, motorcyclists, cyclists, elderly people;
- dangerous road surfaces;
- movements of other traffic;
- weather-related hazards.

▶ Be ready to act in accordance with the M-S-M procedure.

Road layout warning signs

These signs warn of changes in the layout of road(s) ahead. Each road or carriageway is depicted by a solid black line.

Driver's response:

▶ Approach with caution.

▶ Look out for other vehicles that may be approaching or entering the roadway you are travelling on.

▶ Slow down if necessary and obey any other road signs.

Other road layout warning signs

Sharp deviation of route, in direction of arrowheads. These warnings appear at the hazard itself.

Driver's response:

▶ Slow down and drive carefully.

Examples:

 Crossroads ahead

 Side road ahead*

 T-junction

 Staggered junction ahead*

 Adverse camber ahead*

 Double bend ahead, as shown*

 Junction or bend ahead, as shown*

 Junction on a bend*

 Roundabout ahead

Dual carriageway ends ahead

Road narrows ahead, on side shown*

Road narrows on both sides

Two-way trafic on route crossing ahead

Two-way traffic ahead

Plates used with 'Road narrows ahead' signs

| Oncoming vehicles in middle of road | Single file traffic | Single track road |

Examples of 'sharp deviation' signs and accompanying plate:

At a sharp bend in the road

 Block paving on a roundabout

 Reduce speed for road layout change ahead

Road layout warning signs, with test-yourself questions

(Refer to page 40 for the test-yourself instructions.)

Crossroads ahead

The broad black line indicates which road has priority.

Traffic on the other road must give way.

1 **What does this sign mean?**

Select two answers

a There is a crossroads ahead.

b You have priority.

c The cross road has priority.

d Junction ahead with traffic lights.

T-junction ahead

There is a junction ahead where the road does not continue straight ahead.

You will have to turn left or right. Vehicles turning left have priority.

2 **What does this sign mean?**

Select two answers

a Vehicles turning right have priority.

b Vehicles turning left have priority.

c T-junction ahead.

d Workshop at the junction ahead.

Double bend ahead*

The road ahead bends first to one direction and then to the other.

Slow down and drive carefully.

3 **What does this sign mean?**

Select one answer

a Mountain pass ahead.

b Danger! Slippery surface ahead.

c Road ahead curves left, then right.

d Lane change on the road ahead.

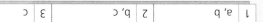

1 a, b   2 b, c   3 c

Roundabout ahead

There is a roundabout at the junction ahead.

Comply with the rules for roundabouts.

Approach with caution and slow down as necessary.

Look out for vehicles approaching from the right.

Comply with lane discipline and any road sign requirements.

4 What does this sign mean?

Select one answer

a Junction ahead.

b Confused motorists ahead.

c Bus terminus ahead.

d Roundabout ahead.

End of dual carriageway ahead

The road becomes a two-way road with traffic moving in both directions.

Keep left and expect oncoming traffic.

5 What does this sign mean and how should you respond?

Select two answers

a You will be sharing the road with oncoming traffic.

b Road becomes very narrow ahead.

c High tunnel entrance ahead.

d End of dual carriageway ahead.

Two-way traffic ahead

The carriageway ahead carries traffic moving in both directions.

Keep well to the left to allow for oncoming traffic.

6 Where would you be likely to see this sign?

Select one answer

a Where there is a bumpy road surface ahead.

b After an 'End of dual carriageway' sign.

c Before two one-way streets.

d Where there will be a reduction in the number of lanes ahead.

Two-way traffic on crossing route ahead

At the junction ahead the cross route carries traffic moving in both directions.

Look to the left and right to check that it is safe to enter or cross the junction.

If turning, be sure to turn into the appropriate lane with the traffic flow.

If turning right, cross the centre line of the cross road before turning.

7 How would you respond to this sign if intending to turn right at the junction?

Select three answers

a Beware of vehicles swerving from left to right.

b Be careful of cross-winds at the junction.

c Watch out for traffic coming from the left and from the right at the junction ahead.

d Comply with any road signs or signals at the junction.

e Pass the centre line of the cross route before making the turn.

Ford ahead

There is a ford ahead, which may contain water or debris.

Slow down and drive carefully, particularly after rainfall.

8 What does this sign mean?

Select one answer

a Caution: puddles on the road ahead.

b Caution: motor vehicle factory ahead.

c Weighbridge ahead. Trucks must stop.

d Caution: there is a stream that crosses the road ahead.

Steep downhill ahead

The road ahead goes downhill steeply.

Prepare to slow down and change to a lower gear if necessary, particularly if driving a heavy vehicle.

Look out for any advisory or regulatory signs.

9 What can you expect when you see this sign?

Select two answers

a Your fuel availability will decrease by 10%.

b You may need to change to a lower gear.

c Steep downhill ahead.

d Steep uphill ahead.

Potential hazard warning signs

These signs warn of potential hazards on or near the road(s) ahead.

Driver's response:

▶ Approach with caution and respond appropriately.

▶ Heed the information or advice on any supplementary advisory plate.

▶ Slow down if necessary and obey any other road signs or signals.

Examples:

Slippery road ahead

Uneven road ahead

Soft verges ahead for distance shown

Risk of falling or fallen rocks ahead

Opening or swing bridge ahead

Loose chippings or stones on the road ahead

Road works ahead

Low-flying aircraft ahead or possible sudden noise

Low-flying helicopters ahead or possible sudden noise

Slow-moving military vehicles likely ahead

Slow-moving lorries likely ahead for distance shown

Slow-moving agricultural vehicles likely ahead

Supervised cattle crossing with lights ahead

Advance warning: supervised cattle crossing ahead

Cattle likely ahead

Cattle grid ahead

Sheep likely ahead

Accompanied horses or ponies likely ahead

Migratory toad crossing ahead

Wild fowl likely ahead

Wild animals likely ahead

Test brakes after crossing a ford or before going down a steep hill

Steep hill upwards ahead

Steep hill downwards ahead

Wild horses likely ahead

Children likely ahead

Plates used with 'steep hill' signs:

Low gear for 1½ miles

Low gear now

Keep in low gear

More hazard warning signs and supplementary plates

End of bridge parapet, wall, tunnel mouth, etc.

Lights: Children likely to be crossing the road ahead

Nearside edge of carriageway (on a dual carriageway, white markers on outside edge, amber on offside edge)

AMBULANCE STATION

STOP when lights show

Ambulance station ahead

250 yds ←

Distance and direction to hazard

400 yds

Distance to hazard

For 2 miles

Distance over which hazard extends

Max speed 20

Recommended maximum speed limit

Weight restriction ahead

Restriction or prohibition ahead, as described

FIRE STATION

STOP when lights show

Fire station ahead

Humped Pelican Crossing

Humped pelican crossing ahead

Elderly people

Elderly people likely ahead

Blind people

Blind people likely ahead

Disabled people

Disabled people likely ahead

Humped Zebra Crossing

Humped zebra crossing ahead

School

Children ahead going to and from school

Playground

Children's playground ahead

Patrol

School patrol crossing ahead

Disabled children

Disabled children likely ahead

Deaf

Deaf children likely ahead

Blind

Blind children likely ahead

Gliders

Gliders likely ahead

Cattle grid

Horse drawn vehicles and animals

Bypass of cattle grid ahead

ANIMAL DISEASE RABIES INFECTED AREA AHEAD

Area ahead infected by animal disease

Warning signs for low bridges and structures

These signs warn of a low bridge or structure ahead, normally with a clearance of less than 16 feet 6 inches (about 5 metres).

Driver's response:

▶ Look well ahead and be prepared to stop and give way to any approaching bus or lorry that may need to be in the centre of the road to clear the bridge safely.

▶ If you are driving a high vehicle, use the advance height guides overhead and on the road surface, if provided, to position your vehicle to pass under the structure safely according to your vehicle's height.

▶ If you are unsure of your vehicle's height, including any loads or antennae, stop safely and check.

▶ If there is any doubt that your vehicle will pass safely under the bridge or structure, take an alternative route by following the 'Overheight Vehicle Divert' arrow sign, or other signs indicating alternative routes.

Examples:

Maximum safe headroom under a bridge or overhead obstruction ahead

Maximum safe headroom under an arch bridge ahead

Additional guidance information plate and road marking ahead of an arch bridge

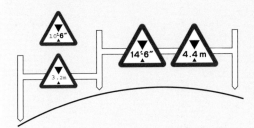

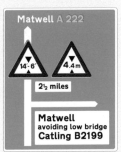

Chord markings indicating varying headroom heights at an arch bridge ahead

Supplementary plate describing height restriction

Black and yellow bands on bridge arches to make sure you see the arch

At or near the bridge or structure itself you are likely to see the same black symbol on a round regulatory sign prohibiting vehicles that exceed that height from passing the sign:

There is a mandatory height restriction ahead

Warning of temporary height restriction at road works ahead

Alternative routes for avoiding the height limit

Warning signs for railway level crossings

These signs warn about a level crossing ahead, and give additional information to prepare the driver for the specific situation at the crossing.

Driver's response:

▶ Prepare to slow down and stop if necessary.

▶ Obey any signals and other instructions at the crossing.

Examples:

Level crossing ahead, without gate or barrier

Safe height beneath electrified cable at the level crossing ahead

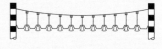

Drivers of LARGE or SLOW VEHICLES must phone and get permission to cross

LARGE means over 55′ long or 9′6″ wide or 38 tonnes total weight SLOW means 5 mph or less

Warning to drivers of large vehicles

Countdown markers showing distance to a concealed level crossing ahead (each bar representing 100 yds)

Audible warning bells to indicate if vehicle height exceeds safe height beneath overhead electrified cable ahead

NEW LEVEL CROSSING CONTROL AHEAD

There is a new method of traffic control at the crossing ahead

---

More hazard warning signs, with test-yourself questions

(Refer to page 40 for the test-yourself instructions.)

Cross-winds ahead

Usually over bridges, after mountain passes or near flat plains.

Expect strong crosswinds ahead. Prepare to slow down if necessary.

Hold the steering wheel firmly.

10 What does this sign mean?

Select one answer

a Beware of storms ahead.

b Slow down – airport ahead.

c Expect strong crosswinds ahead.

d Flags ahead indicate off-road service area.

Anti-speed humps ahead

Usually in a residential area where traffic calming is necessary.

There are humps on the road ahead to slow traffic down.

Drive slowly at a safe speed, and obey any speed limit signs.

11 What does this sign mean?

Humps for ½ mile

Select two answers

a Bumpy road ahead for half a mile; slow down.

b Humpback bridge half a mile ahead. Keep left.

c Traffic calming humps on road ahead, for half a mile.

d Slow down to a safe speed.

e Mini-roundabout half a mile ahead.

10 c   11 c, d

Hump bridge ahead

There is a hump bridge ahead, where vision ahead is obscured by the hump.

Slow down, beware of pedestrians and of oncoming vehicles hidden from view.

Move into the middle of the road for a better view.

If necessary, sound your horn as a warning.

12 What should you do when you see this sign?

Select two answers

a Keep far to the left to avoid oncoming traffic.

b Stop and wait until the bridge is clear.

c Move to the middle of the road for a better view.

d Prepare to sound your horn if necessary.

Risk of ice ahead

There is a possibility of ice on the road surface ahead.

Reduce speed gradually, as stopping distances are increased by up to ten times when it's icy.

To avoid tyres losing grip, don't brake or steer harshly.

13 What does this sign mean?

Select one answer

a Multi-exit roundabout ahead.

b Turn on your air conditioner through hot patch ahead.

c Risk of ice on the road ahead.

d Caution: windmills near road ahead.

Danger ahead

There is likely to be a dangerous situation ahead.

A supplementary plate may indicate the nature of the danger – e.g. potholes, accident, flood.

Drive carefully and be ready for any dangerous situation.

14 What does this sign mean?

Select one answer

a Wake up! Falling asleep is dangerous!

b Danger ahead.

c Traffic lights ahead.

d Road closed ahead.

ROAD SIGNS, SIGNALS AND MARKINGS

12 c, d   13 c   14 b

Tunnel ahead

The road ahead passes through a tunnel.

Slow down and prepare to switch on your headlights.

Be ready to adjust to sudden darkness in the tunnel.

15 **What does this sign mean?**

Select one answer

a Tunnel ahead; turn on your headlights.

b Low bridge ahead; slow down.

c Historical monument close to roadside ahead.

d Railway station ahead; look out for pedestrians.

Quayside or river bank ahead

The road ahead leads to or near a quayside or river bank.

The road could be wet or slippery.

16 **What does this sign mean?**

Select one answer

a Car ferry ahead.

b Be careful of going over the edge into a river.

c Dumping area for old, trashed vehicles.

d Quayside or river bank ahead.

Pedestrian crossing ahead

Adjust speed as necessary and keep a lookout for pedestrians about to enter the crossing.

Check the nearby pavements for anyone who looks as if they might step into the road.

17 **What does this sign mean?**

Select one answer

a School crossing patrol ahead.

b Fitness walking track ahead.

c Pedestrian zone ahead – no vehicles permitted.

d Pedestrian crossing ahead.

Pedestrians in the road ahead

There may be pedestrians walking along the road ahead. Drive very carefully.

Check in your mirrors before moving out to leave plenty of room when you pass any pedestrians.

Be particularly careful when approaching a bend in the road.

18 How would you respond to this sign?

Select three answers

a Slow down for school children crossing.

b Be careful when nearing a bend.

c Prepare to move across to the right.

d Slow down near school ahead.

e Take extra care.

f Stop your vehicle and start walking.

Level crossing ahead, with gate or barrier

Warns of a railway crossing ahead, with no attendant or signals, only a gate or barrier.

Prepare to slow down to stop at the crossing, look both ways, and listen for rail traffic.

Once you're at the crossing, use the roadside phone (if provided) to check with the signal operator that it is safe to cross.

19 What does this sign mean?

Select one answer

a Motor gate ahead.

b Level crossing ahead, with gate or barrier.

c Cattle grid on the road ahead.

d Road closed ahead. Take an alternative route.

Trams crossing the road ahead

There are trams running on rails across the road ahead.

Slow down and look out for trams and passengers.

Be particularly careful at junctions where trams cross.

20 What does this sign mean?

Select one answer

a Rail crossing ahead.

b Railway museum ahead.

c Trams crossing ahead.

d Area ahead reserved for trams only.

18 b, c, e   19 b   20 c

Pedal cycle route ahead

There is a cycle route ahead where cyclists are likely to be riding.

Look out for people on cycles and for cyclists moving on to the main road.

21 **What does this sign mean?**

Select one answer

a Cycle repair shop ahead.

b Cycles prohibited on road ahead.

c Cycles must be pushed across the road ahead.

d There is a cycle route ahead.

Road works ahead

There are road works being done ahead, or a temporary obstruction on the road.

Slow down and comply with any signs at the road works.

(See Chapter 13 for the signs to be expected at road works.)

22 **How should you respond to this sign?**

Select one answer

a Slow down for grave diggers ahead.

b Slow down for road works ahead.

c Stop and clear snow before continuing.

d Snow clearing being done ahead.

Traffic signals ahead not in use

The traffic signals ahead are not in use.

Drive carefully and look out for other road signs or hand signals.

23 **What does this sign mean?**

Select one answer

a Traffic signals out of use.

b No traffic signals used on this road.

c Traffic signals turned off during the day.

d All of the above.

9 Regulatory signs

Regulatory signs regulate traffic flow. They must always be obeyed and failure to do so can result in a heavy penalty. There are three basic categories of regulatory signs and each category conveys a specific *type* of message to the motorist.

Red odd-shaped signs tell you where to stop or give way.

Red circle signs tell you what you **may not do**, or specify a **particular limit** (e.g. speed limit, height limit).

Blue circle signs tell you what you **must or may do**. Some blue command signs are rectangular in shape.

General response to all regulatory signs:

▶ Obey each sign.

Red signs for stopping and giving way (green for 'Go')

Examples:

Stop

Give way

Proceed (manually operated sign at road works)

Red circle signs prohibiting access beyond the sign

Examples:

No entry to any vehicles (displayed by a police or traffic warden)

No entry to any vehicles (displayed by a school crossing patrol)

No entry to any vehicles

No vehicles or cycling allowed

No motor vehicles allowed

No motorcycles allowed

No motor vehicles allowed (except motorcycles without sidecars)

No horse-drawn vehicles allowed

No horses allowed at all

No pedestrians allowed

No articulated vehicles allowed

More red circle signs prohibiting access beyond the sign

Examples:

No vehicles over the maximum
height shown are allowed

Advance warning of a mandatory
height restriction ahead

No vehicles over the maximum
width shown are allowed

No vehicles over the maximum
length shown are allowed
(includes any trailer combination)

No goods vehicles over
maximum weight shown are
allowed (gross weight in tonnes)

No vehicles with
over eight passenger
seats are allowed

No vehicles over
maximum gross weight
shown are allowed

Supplementary plates for vehicle prohibition signs

**Except for
loading by**

Except for loading and unloading goods vehicles

**Except for
access**

Except where there is no other
route giving access to property
adjacent to the road

**Except empty
vehicles**

No vehicles over maximum gross
weight shown, except if the
vehicle is empty

**No motor vehicles,
cycles, animals,
pedestrians
on mown verge**

No access allowed, as shown on the sign

**No vehicles,
10am - 4 pm
except for
access**

During the times shown, except for access

**Play Street
8 am to sunset
except for
access**

Except for access

Red circle signs prohibiting certain actions

Examples:

No U-turn
allowed here

No right turn
allowed

No left turn
allowed

No overtaking
allowed

Give way to oncoming
vehicles (don't force your way
through a narrow road)

No stopping on main
carriageway at any time
for any reason

Don't drive faster than
the speed shown in mph
(speed limit sign)

The speed limit is now the
national speed limit
applicable to the type of
road and class of traffic

Red circle signs prohibiting or restricting waiting or loading

Waiting restrictions normally apply to the highway as well as the verges and footways where the sign is in force. The regulatory signs are usually on a board containing additional information, and normally accompanied by yellow lines along the edge of the carriageway (see Chapter 14).

Always comply with the regulatory signs and accompanying restrictions.

Examples:

No waiting

Waiting prohibited 24 hours a day, 7 days a week, for at least 4 consecutive months

Accompanying road marking for 24/7 waiting restriction

Waiting prohibited for a shorter period, as indicated (arrow indicates where restriction begins)

Accompanying road marking for shorter waiting restrictions

Entrance to meter zone

Entrance to voucher parking zone

End of controlled or voucher parking zone

At the entry to a zone where waiting by certain vehicle classes is restricted as shown

Waiting by certain vehicle classes is restricted as shown and in the direction shown

Loading areas

No waiting, except by permitted vehicles loading or offloading

Stopping allowed only for loading at the marked loading bay

Loading restrictions

No loading at all

No loading in the direction of the arrows, within times stated

Clearways

You may not stop in a clearway. 'Clearway' may be included on boards with additional information such as times during which the clearway is in operation, or exempted vehicles. Some examples are given below.

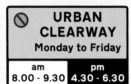

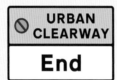

Signs cancelling a prohibition, restriction or instruction

Where a restriction or prohibition no longer applies, a 'greyed-out' version of the sign is displayed.

Examples:

End of goods vehicles prohibition

End of speed limit zone and return to limit shown in red circle

End of parking/loading/other zones

Blue command-type signs

Examples:

Proceed straight ahead
(one-way traffic)

Proceed left only*

Pass to either the
left or the right

Pass to the left*

Mini-roundabout

Turn left ahead

Turn right ahead

Shared route for
pedal cycles and
pedestrians only

Separated track and path
for pedal cycles and
pedestrians only

Route for pedal
cycles only

Plates supplementing 'turn' signs:

**Dual
carriageway**

One way

Travel at the speed
shown, or faster
(minimum speed
allowed)

Route for trams only

Route for buses and
cycles only

Blue rectangular signs for parking

Examples:

Vehicles may park partially
on the verge or footway

Vehicles may park wholly
on the verge or footway

Supplementary plate for
parking signs:

6 pm - 8 am

Times during which sign applies

Blue signs showing the end of an applicable zone

Examples:

End of a minimum speed
requirement

End of area where
vehicles may park wholly
on the verge or footway

Regulatory signs at pedestrian zones

Some busy pedestrian areas, such as a street with shops, may be designated as pedestrian zones, with signs to indicate any restrictions applying to motor vehicles. Additional information may be given too, such as when the restrictions apply, and which if any vehicles are exempted.

Be sure to comply with any regulatory sign restrictions or prohibitions.

Examples:

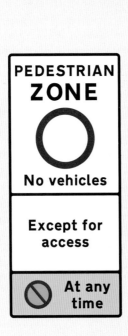

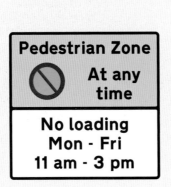

Regulatory signs, with test-yourself questions

Stop

Appears at a junction.

Stop before the white 'Stop' line on the road.

Look in all directions. If the road is clear, proceed.

1 What must you do at this sign?

Select one answer

a Stop, even if the road is clear of approaching traffic. ☐

b Stop only if traffic is approaching. ☐

c Stop only if there are pedestrians waiting to cross. ☐

d Stop only if a red signal light is showing. ☐

No entry for vehicles

No vehicles allowed.

Don't drive beyond this sign; take an alternative route.

2 Which sign means vehicles may not enter?

Select one answer

a   ☐   b   ☐

c   ☐   d   ☐

No motor vehicles allowed

No vehicles allowed.

Area set aside for pedestrians.

Don't drive beyond this sign; take an alternative route.

3 What does this sign mean?

Select two answers

a Area set aside for pedestrians. ☐

b Only motorcycles and cars allowed. ☐

c No motor vehicles allowed. ☐

d Parking zone for motor vehicles. ☐

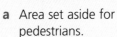

ROAD SIGNS, SIGNALS AND MARKINGS

No motorcycles allowed

Motorcycles are not allowed.

Motorcyclists must not ride beyond this sign; take an alternative route.

4 What does this sign mean?

Select one answer

a Motorcycle races ahead.

b No motorcycles allowed.

c Motorcycle route only.

d Motorcycle rally in progress.

No overtaking allowed

Don't overtake any vehicles beyond this sign.

Be patient if you're behind a slow-moving vehicle.

To overtake, wait until the restriction is cancelled.

5 Which sign means you may not overtake?

Select one answer

a

b

c

d

One-way traffic

You are entering a one-way street.

Travel only in the direction of the arrow.

Use the most appropriate lane for your destination.

6 Which sign indicates that you are entering a one-way street?

Select one answer

a

b

c

d

Turn at junction ahead*

Appears before a junction.

You must turn in the direction of the arrow at the junction ahead.

You may not proceed in any other direction.

7 What does this sign mean?

Select one answer

a Sharp left turn ahead. ☐

b Turn right at the junction ahead. ☐

c Road ahead curves to the right. ☐

d Parking available on the right. ☐

Give way to oncoming vehicles

Appears where there is not enough space for two vehicles to pass safely (a narrow bridge, road works or obstruction).

Yield to any oncoming traffic at the narrow section of the road, and don't force your way through.

Proceed only when the road is clear.

8 How should you respond to this sign?

Select two answers

a You should have priority over oncoming traffic. ☐

b Give way to oncoming traffic. ☐

c Expect two-way traffic ahead. ☐

d Oncoming traffic has priority. ☐

Give way to trams

Give way to trams at the level crossing.

There are no barriers or gates.

Proceed only when safe to do so.

9 Where would you find this sign and how would you respond?

Select two answers

a At an uncontrolled railway level crossing without barriers. ☐

b At a tram level crossing without barriers or gates. ☐

c Give way to trains. ☐

d Give way to trams. ☐

e Trams must give way. ☐

Mini-roundabout

Appears at a junction.

Slow down and approach with caution.

Look out for other vehicles approaching or on the roundabout.

Signal your intention early enough.

Obey any direction signs.

10 What does this sign mean?

Select one answer

a Mini-roundabout.

b Roundabout.

c Traffic circle.

d Bus terminus.

Pass either to left or to right

In a one-way street having more than one lane.

Pass to the left or to the right to get into the appropriate lane for your destination.

11 What does this sign mean?

Select one answer

a Extra lanes ahead. Slow down.

b Be careful of tram rails.

c Turn your headlights to dipped beam.

d Pass to the left or the right in the same direction.

Parking allowed on verge

Vehicles may park wholly on the verge or footway at any time.

12 What does this sign mean?

Select one answer

a Parking garage for cars only.

b Penalties imposed for parking on the verge.

c Pedestrians and cars have access here.

d Vehicles may park wholly on the verge or footway at any time.

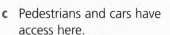

No waiting allowed

A temporary portable sign (on a yellow board) to prohibit waiting.

Don't stop or wait in the area governed by the sign.

13 What does this temporary sign mean?

Select one answer

a   No entry to vehicles.

b   No entry to vehicles and pedestrians.

c   No waiting allowed.

d   No through road.

National speed limit applies

The national maximum speed limit, for the type of road and the class of vehicle, applies beyond this sign.

Drive within the speed limit for the road and your class of vehicle.

14 What is the maximum speed limit for a car travelling on a single carriageway where this sign is displayed?

Select one answer

a   The national maximum speed limit, in this case 60 mph.

b   The national minimum speed limit.

c   The sign means 'No entry'.

d   No speed limit applies. This sign cancels any speed limit.

Minimum speed allowed

You must travel at or faster than the speed indicated.

If it is unsafe or impractical to do so, you may be exempted.

15 Which sign indicates the slowest speed at which you may travel?

Select one answer

a   b

c   d

Entrance to speed-limit zone

Entrance to a zone with traffic-calming measures and a speed limit of 20 mph.

Don't drive faster than the speed limit.

16 What does this sign mean?

Select one answer

a Start of speed-limit zone with traffic-calming measures. ☐

b Bee farming. Speed limit applies. ☐

c Pedestrian zone. Adhere to speed limit. ☐

d 20-tonne lorries prohibited in this zone. ☐

End of speed-limit zone

The speed-limit zone ends here.

You may now drive up to the maximum speed indicated.

17 What does this sign mean?

Select three answers

a The lower speed limit no longer applies. ☐

b Speed limit is now 30 mph. ☐

c End of 20 mph zone. ☐

d Minimum speed now raised to 30 mph. ☐

Maximum vehicle height allowed

Vehicles whose maximum height exceeds the limit shown must not pass the sign.

They must take an alternative route.

18 Which signs mean that vehicles exceeding the height shown must not pass this sign?

Select two answers

a ☐

b ☐

c ☐

d ☐

No vehicles with over 8 seats allowed

Vehicles with more than 8 passenger seats, and local buses, must not pass this sign.

They must take an alternative route.

19 Which vehicles may not proceed beyond this sign?

Select two answers

a Long vehicles.

b Buses with more than 8 passenger seats.

c Buses with more than 12 passenger seats.

d Local buses.

Clearway: no stopping allowed

This is a clearway and must be kept clear at all times.

Don't stop on the main carriageway at any time, for any reason.

You may stop only at a layby.

20 What does this sign mean?

Select one answer

a No entry to any vehicles at any time.

b Dangerous junction.

c Give way to trains at level crossing.

d No stopping at any time.

Route for trams only

The route is for trams only.

No other vehicles may drive on this route.

Don't block any tram route, as trams move quickly and quietly, and are unable to swerve as they run on rails.

21 What does this sign mean?

Select one answer

a Stopping place for trams only.

b Route for trams only.

c Only trams prohibited.

d Only buses allowed.

Route for buses and pedal cycles only

The route is for buses and pedal cycles only.

No other vehicles may drive on this route.

22 What does this sign mean?

Select one answer

a Stopping place for buses and pedal cycles only.

b Route for buses and pedal cycles only.

c Pedal cycles have priority over buses.

d Only trams and pedal cycles allowed.

Contra-flow bus lane

The lane on the right is for oncoming buses.

Don't use the lane for parking or overtaking.

Stay within the two left lanes only.

23 What does this sign mean?

Select one answer

a Don't drive in the contra-flow bus lane.

b Right lane leads to bus station.

c Buses should use the right-hand lane only.

d Overtake buses on the left.

Traffic signals

Traffic signals are used to regulate the flow of traffic, pedestrians and cyclists. They take the form of traffic lights and overhead light signals.

In many situations there are 'duplicate signals' situated on the opposite side of a junction in case the primary signals are out of order. Always comply with traffic signals, including the duplicate signals if the primary signals are not working.

Traffic light signals, with test-yourself questions

Red disc light

Stop before the white Stop line on the road.

Proceed only when the green light is displayed, and only if it is safe to do so.

Look out for pedestrians still crossing, and vehicles still passing through the junction.

1 **What must you do when the red light is on?**

Select three answers

a Slow down and proceed only if safe to do so.

b Stop before the white Stop line.

c Wait for the green light before proceeding.

d Give way to any pedestrians still crossing the junction.

e Once the green light is on, you have right of way over any pedestrians.

Amber disc light

Stop before the white Stop line, unless it is unsafe to do so.

If you have already crossed the Stop line when the amber light comes on, you may continue if stopping might cause an accident.

2 **If the amber light goes on as you approach a junction, which two statements apply?**

Select two answers

a You must stop before the Stop line, unless it is unsafe to do so.

b You can zip through quickly before the red light comes on if there is a clear way.

c Treat it as a 'Give way' sign.

d You may continue if you have already crossed the Stop line and if stopping might cause an accident.

Red and amber disc lights

Stop before the white Stop line on the road.

Proceed only when the green light is displayed, and only if it is safe to do so.

Look out for pedestrians still crossing, and vehicles still passing through the junction.

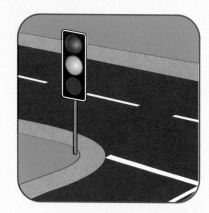

3 **What must you do when the red and amber lights are on?**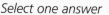

Select one answer

a Slow down and proceed only if safe to do so.

b Increase speed to get through before it turns red.

c Stop before the Stop line and wait for green.

d Slow down and give way to crossing traffic.

Green disc light

Proceed if the way is clear and it is safe to do so.

Look out for pedestrians still crossing, and vehicles still passing through the junction.

Check for cyclists and let them move off safely.

If the light has been green for some time, it might be about to change, so be prepared to stop.

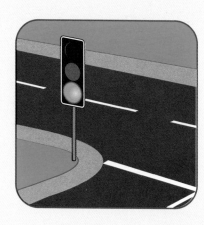

4 **What must you do when the green light is on?**

Select one answer

a Slow down and proceed only if it is safe to do so.

b Proceed if the way is clear.

c Speed up to get clear before the lights change.

d Stop, give way to pedestrians, then continue.

Green disc with regulatory sign

A regulatory sign might be added to qualify the accompanying light signal.

In this example, you may proceed on green, but may not turn left.

Obey any accompanying road sign at a traffic light.

5 **What does this traffic light mean?**

Select one answer

a The 'No left turn' sign overrules the green 'Go' signal.

b The light is green, so proceed.

c You may proceed but may not turn left.

d Trams may not turn left. Other vehicles may proceed.

One way only

A blue command sign may be used to emphasize the message of the green arrow signal.

The road at the junction is a one-way road to the left.

When the green arrow light is on, vehicles must proceed only in the direction of the arrow(s).

6 What does this traffic signal mean?

Select one answer

a Proceed straight ahead.

b Proceed to the left only.

c You may not turn left.

d Bus lane to the left.

Green arrow light

Vehicles may proceed in the direction of the green arrow, if it is safe to do so, irrespective of whether a red 'Stop' light is displayed.

A regulatory sign may accompany the green arrow for emphasis.

7 What does this traffic light mean?

Select one answer

a When the disc light turns green, you must turn left.

b Stop and wait.

c The cross road is a one-way street to the left.

d Stop before the Stop line, except if turning left.

Green disc light, with green arrow light

When both are on together, you may proceed straight ahead or turn right.

Oncoming traffic is being held up by a red 'Stop' light.

8 What does this traffic light mean?

Select two answers

a You may proceed straight ahead.

b You may turn right, but give way to oncoming traffic.

c You may turn right. Oncoming traffic must wait.

d The cross road is a one-way street to the right.

ROAD SIGNS, SIGNALS AND MARKINGS

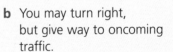
6 b   7 d   8 a, c

Overhead lane control signals

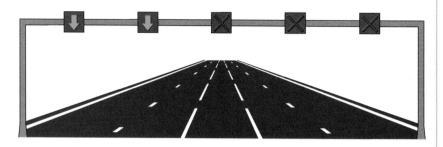

Lane control signals may be erected on an overhead gantry across the road. They regulate which lanes may be used, according to the current traffic flow situation.

Lane closed to traffic facing the signal   Lane available to traffic facing the signal   Lane closed ahead. Move to next lane on left

Motorway signals

▶ Look out for motorway signals that warn you of danger ahead.

▶ Signals on the central reservation apply to all lanes.

▶ Overhead signals may apply to separate lanes.

☀ Amber flashing signals warn of a hazard ahead.

  – Adjust your speed according to the signal and look out for danger on the road ahead.

  – Increase your speed again once you have passed a non-flashing signal or an 'All clear' signal, and it is safe to do so.

☀ Red flashing lights mean you must not proceed beyond the signal. A signal in the central reservation applies to all lanes. A signal above a lane applies to that lane only.

For more information and test-yourself questions, see Chapter 15, 'Motorway signs and signals'.

Tram signs and signals

Trams (electric vehicles that move along fixed rails) often share roads used by other vehicles and pedestrians. Because they are unable to change course, the area they move along (the 'swept path') **must be kept clear at all times**. So that the swept path can be easily identified, it often has a different colour, surface texture or markings from the road to be used by other vehicles.

The following signs and signals apply only to trams. However, for safety on the roads it is advisable that all road users know and understand what these signs and signals mean.

Signs for tram drivers only

Diamond-shaped signs are applicable to tram drivers only.

 Speed limit

Signals for tram drivers only

Signals for tram drivers are mounted to the right of normal traffic lights.

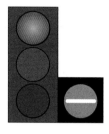

Stop

Proceed ahead   Proceed left

Proceed right   Stop, except if unsafe to stop

Tram signs and signals for pedestrians

The lights flash to indicate that a tram is coming

Be careful of approaching trams

11 Signals by drivers and officials

Indicators and hand signals are used by drivers to indicate the driver's intentions. Hand signals by officials are used to control traffic flow. Always obey traffic signals given by authorized persons such as police officers or traffic wardens, and others authorized to direct traffic in specific situations.

Signals to other road users

Direction indicator signals*

Indicates intention to move or turn in the direction shown

Braking light signals

Indicates intention to slow
down or stop

Reversing light signals

Indicates intention to reverse

Arm signals

Indicates intention to move
to or turn left

Indicates intention to
move to or turn right

Indicates intention to
slow down or stop

Giving signals

- Before signalling, make sure that it is safe to signal.
- Signal early enough to warn other road users.
- Give clear signals using direction indicators, brake lights or hand signals.
- Don't signal too early, as this can confuse other road users.
- Signal your intention before:
  – stopping;
  – moving off;
  – changing direction.
- Cancel the signal after use, and make sure it is cancelled.
- If necessary, use an arm signal for emphasis, for example in bright sunlight when the indicators are not so visible.
- Signalling does not give you automatic right of way.

Giving signals

The examiner will watch how you signal as you drive. To let other road users know what you intend doing, you must always signal your intention to move off, change direction, or stop.

Things you must do

- Give proper signals as required.
- Make sure that the signal is cancelled after use.

Some don'ts

- Don't signal carelessly or unnecessarily.
- Don't wave pedestrians across the road.

Obeying signals

- Obey all signals given by:
  – police officers;
  – traffic wardens;
  – school crossing patrols;
  – traffic lights;
  – traffic signs giving orders;
  – temporary signals and signs.
- If instructed by the police, pull over and stop where it is safe to do so, and switch off your engine.
- The police may direct you to stop by:
  – flashing blue lights or headlights; and/or
  – sounding a siren or horn; and/or
  – pointing and/or flashing their left indicator.

Obeying signals

When the test starts, the examiner will direct you to follow a particular road. You will be asked to turn at junctions where you must respond to road signs, lane markings, signals and direction signs.

Things you must do

- Obey signals given by police officers, traffic wardens and school crossing patrols.
- Take extra care where there are reduced speed limits, speed restriction humps and width restrictions.

Signals by authorized persons

Traffic must stop

Applies to traffic approaching the officer from the front

Applies to traffic approaching the officer from both front and behind

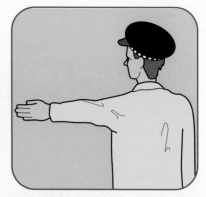

Applies to traffic approaching the officer from behind

Traffic must proceed

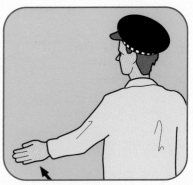

From the front

From the side

From behind

Traffic must stop at school crossing

Driver arm signals to officials controlling traffic

I want to go straight ahead

I want to turn right

I want to turn left

Vehicles with flashing amber lights

◗ Approach these vehicles cautiously as they could be moving slowly or stationary.

Progress test

Signals by drivers and officials

The number in brackets at the end of each question indicates how many correct answers you should mark.

1 What is the first thing you must do when you want to turn right? (1)

a Move into the right-hand lane to position your vehicle correctly.

b Signal your intention.

c Flick your indicator once to make sure it's working.

d Make sure it is safe to signal.

2 When should you signal your intention? (3)

a Before stopping.

b Before slowing down.

c Before changing direction.

d Before moving off.

3 When should you use an arm signal? (1)

a Before leaving a motorway.

b At night.

c In bright sunlight.

d Never.

4 Which statement is wrong? (1)

a Signalling gives you automatic right of way.

b Signal early enough to warn other road users.

c Don't signal so early that it could confuse other road users.

d Give clear signals.

5 Which statement is wrong? (1)

a Obey the signals given by police officers.

b Obey the signals given by a postman on duty.

c Obey the signals given by traffic wardens.

d Obey the signals given by school crossing patrols.

6 What kind of road signs have a circular shape? (1)

a Signs that give direction.

b Signs that give warnings.

c Signs that give information.

d Signs that give orders.

7 What kind of road signs have a triangular shape? (1)

a Signs that give direction.

b Signs that give warnings.

c Signs that give information.

d Signs that indicate non-primary routes.

8 What kind of road signs are green with a rectangular shape? (1)

a Signs that give direction.

b Signs that give warnings.

c Signs that give information.

d Signs that indicate non-primary routes.

9 What kind of situation could a triangular sign indicate? (1)

a Children or animals running on to the road.

b A speed limit applies here.

c Motorcycles are not allowed.

d None of these.

10 You should look in the mirrors before: (3)

a Signalling.

b Closing your door.

c Moving off.

d Changing speed.

11 Why should fog lights not be used when visibility is good? (1)

a Because they will not be easily seen.

b Because it is illegal to do so.

c Because they can appear to be brake lights.

d Because it wastes battery power unnecessarily.

12 What are the main risks when passing a stationary bus, coach or tram? (3)

a Its width could cause you to collide with it.

b Pedestrians might walk into the road.

c It might suddenly move into your path.

d Pedestrians might run across the road to get on board.

7 b	8 a	9 a	10 a, c, d	11 c	12 b, c, d
1 d	2 a, c b	3 c	4 a	5 b	6 d

Direction and general information signs

These signs offer route guidance and other useful information to make travelling easier and more interesting.

Generally, they are rectangular in shape; some direction signs are shaped as a 'fingerboard' – a rectangular board with a pointed end representing an arrowhead to indicate the direction to the location shown. The colour combinations vary according to the nature of the information being given.

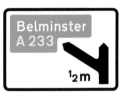

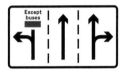

If you understand the meanings of the various colour combinations, and also the different symbols used, you will easily be able to interpret at a glance the meanings of direction, guidance and general information signs.

Signs using symbols

As with warning and regulatory signs, information is often given symbolically rather than in words. The colour of the background will vary according to the type of route, but the symbols remain the same.

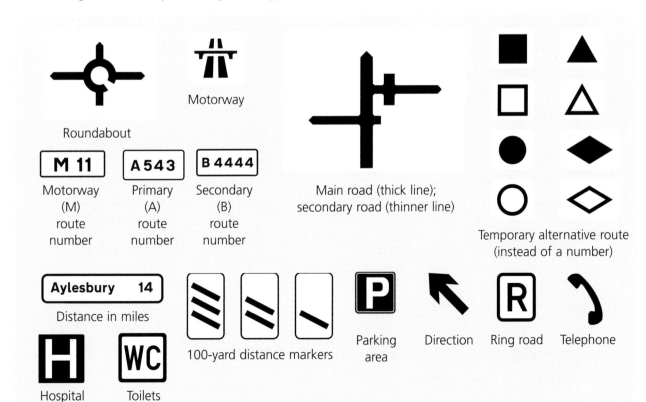

Facility for disabled

Restaurant

Light refreshments

Hotel/motel

Fuel

Tourist information

Railway station

Goods vehicles

Tourist sign symbols (on brown background)

Picnic area

Youth hostel

Camping site

Caravan site

Tourist information point

Castle

Historic house

National Trust property

Zoo

Wildlife park

Country park

Air museum

Pleasure or theme park

Agricultural museum

Motor museum

Roman remains

Shire horse centre

Vineyard

English Heritage

Flower garden

Nature reserve

Viewing point

Prehistoric site or monument

Industrial heritage museum

Old railway

General attraction in England

General attraction in Scotland

General attraction in Wales

Route direction signs

These signs indicate a direction, or an alternative direction, to a location such as a town, airport, tourist attraction, industrial area, service area, parking area, etc. There are two types of routes: primary routes, and non-primary (or 'other') routes.

	On primary routes	On non-primary routes
Board colour:	Green	White
Text and border:	White	Black
Route numbers:	Gold	Black

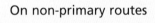

Coloured panels

Where the destination shown is on a different type of route from the one you're travelling on, a coloured panel indicates the importance of the other route.

On primary routes / **On non-primary routes**

The other route (blue panel) is a motorway (where motorway regulations will apply from the point of entry)

Blue panel / Blue panel

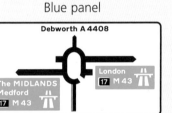

The other route (green panel) is a primary route

Green panel

The other route (white panel) is a non-primary route

White panel

Junction names

Sometimes the name of the junction is shown at the top of the sign, above a horizontal line.

On primary routes

On non-primary routes

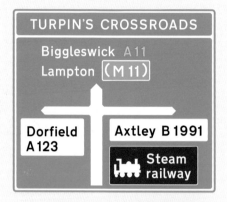

Junction arrow types

On an overhead direction sign the type of arrow indicates the road layout beyond the junction.

An inclined arrow means all lanes continue straight ahead, and there is no loss of lane after the separate junction.

A downward arrow means a loss of lane beyond the junction. Select your destination and move into the correct lane before the exit junction.

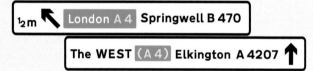

Inclined arrow = no loss of lane

Downward arrow = loss of lane

At a junction turn-off

These signs indicate where to turn off, and are colour-coded according to the route type leading to the destination shown.

To a primary route

Market Walborough B 486 7

To a non-primary route

Route confirmation

After a junction there may be a sign to confirm the route you're on, and the distances in miles to the main destinations ahead.

B 4040 (A 41)

Potten End 2
Gaddesden 3
Aylesbury 14

Recommended route for lorry drivers

These signs are on a black background.

On primary routes

On non-primary routes

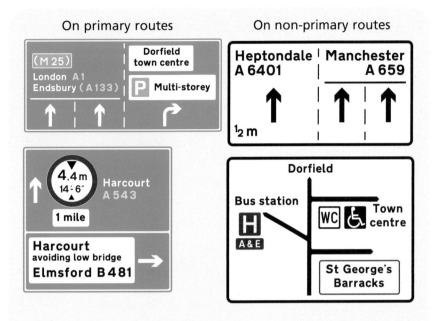

Lane and other information

Advance signs may indicate which lanes to use for the destinations shown. Other information may also be shown – e.g. car park, regulatory or warning sign for route shown, etc.

Ring roads

A ring road bypasses a town centre. These are indicated on advance direction signs and may be confirmed by repeater signs along the ring road route.

Primary ring road repeater sign

Non-primary ring road repeater sign

Town or village bypass

Where the primary route bypasses a town or village, the town name is shown on a white panel.

Countdown markers

These indicate the distance to the start of a deceleration lane leaving the primary route. Each bar represents 100 yards.

Temporary direction signs

Black and yellow signs are used to give directions for an alternative route when a section of a motorway or other main road is temporarily closed to traffic.

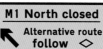

Where the alternative route is difficult to follow without help, a particular symbol is used on the direction sign to identify the route that should be taken – in this example, a diamond shape.

Repeater signs showing the same symbol appear along the temporary route to confirm that you are on the correct route, and to give guidance.

Other examples of repeater signs

More examples of temporary direction signs:

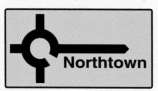

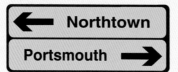

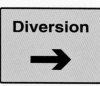

Tourist signs

Examples:

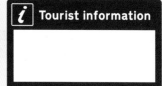

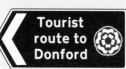

Emergency signs

For emergency vehicles:

To a temporary incident control point

Emergency Vehicles

To a permanent rendezvous point

F.R.P. No.1 — To a permanent fire rendezvous point

Emergency telephone:

For pedestrians:

To an emergency pedestrian exit in a tunnel

Parking ahead for use of the emergency telephone only

Parking direction/ information signs

Parking available

Parking place 1 mile ahead

Parking for only the vehicle type shown

Parking place for 250 vehicles

Park and ride scheme 300 yards ahead

Parking place for lorries only, 1 mile ahead. Toilet and phone also available

Other direction signs

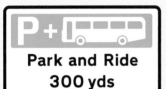
To a Ministry of Defence establishment

To a Department of Transport testing station for goods vehicles

Fingerboard direction sign for minor rural roads

Direction signs for pedestrians and cyclists

Signs for pedestrians and cyclists do not apply to motor vehicles, but for road safety reasons it is advisable that drivers know what these signs mean.

Direction signs depicting a pedestrian symbol or showing the yellow waymark arrow indicate a route specifically for pedestrians. Similarly, cycle routes are depicted by a pedal cycle symbol.

Information signs

These signs give useful information for road users and pedestrians. Most of these signs are blue rectangular boards with the information in white. Signs specifically for drivers of goods vehicles are usually in black on a yellow background.

Information for pedestrians

Ramped pedestrian entrance

Stepped pedestrian entrance

One-way traffic as depicted*

Be careful of buses and pedal cycles from the right*

Be careful of buses from the right*

Be careful of cyclists to the right*

* Denotes there may be left, right and straight-ahead versions.

Information for pedal cyclists

Recommended route for pedal cyclists

Pedal cycle lane or crossing at junction ahead

With-flow pedal cycle lane ahead

With-flow pedal cycle lane

End of cycle route

Pedal cyclists must dismount after cycle lane or route stops

The 'no through route' does not apply to pedal cyclists

Parking place for pedal cycles

Information about vehicle checks

VEHICLE EXCISE LICENCE CHECK

VEHICLE CONDITION INSPECTION

Vehicles will be stopped

Information about police presence

Temporary police warnings

Information about hospitals

No accident or emergency facilities

With accident and emergency facilities

82

Information about goods vehicle checks

GOODS VEHICLES STOP if directed

Department of Transport
CHECK POINT AHEAD

Leave m'way if directed

Keep to left lane

Check Point

All goods vehicles

GET IN LANE

Commercial vehicle Check Point ½ m

GET IN LANE

Goods vehicle Check Point ½ m

Enter Check Point if directed

Goods vehicle restrictions END

Goods vehicles being spot-checked. Follow directions and keep in lane indicated

Information about traffic surveys in progress

SLOW CENSUS POINT

CENSUS STOP if directed

STOP AT CENSUS POINT

CENSUS POINT

Vehicles may be stopped at the census point

Information about road layout and lane control

Dual carriageway 2 miles ahead

Distance to start of dual carriageway ahead

Dual carriageway ahead

Dual carriageway begins here

Dual carriageway for ½ mile

Short dual carriageway section begins here

No through road straight ahead for vehicles

No through road to the left for vehicles

Single track road with passing places

Wide enough for only one vehicle, but there are passing places at intervals

Unsuitable for motor vehicles

This sign may also specify a vehicle type

Number of lanes reduced ahead (non-primary road)

Number of lanes reduced ahead (primary road)

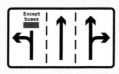

Only buses may proceed straight ahead in the left lane; other vehicles using this lane must turn left

PASSING PLACE

Indicates a passing place on a narrow road

Lane control ahead

Lane control

Lane control 50 yards

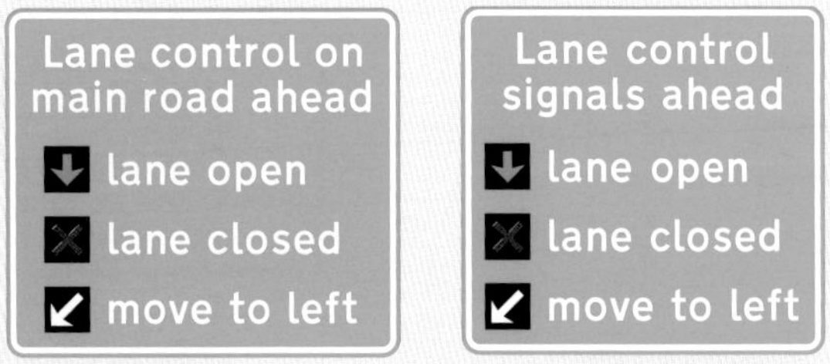

Lane control on main road ahead
- lane open
- lane closed
- move to left

Lane control signals ahead
- lane open
- lane closed
- move to left

Lane control ahead, with meanings of the various overhead lane control signals

End of lane control section   End of lane control

Information about parking areas

 Disc Zone — P Mon - Sat 8 am - 6 pm 30 mins No return within 1 hour

 P Pay at meter ← → Display ticket

P Pay here at meter Display ticket

 P Mon - Sat 9 am - 6 pm Voucher parking only 2 hour limit

 P Have you paid and displayed?

 P Mon - Sat 8 am - 6 pm 20 mins No return within 40 mins

 P Disabled badge holders only

 P Permit holders only

 P Resident permit holders only — A B C

Information about services available (See also Chapter 15 on motorway signs.)

 ↖ Services — WC ⛽ 🍴 ♿ i

 Services ½ m 🚚 Lorries only WC ⛽ ☕ i not 24 hrs

 ↖ Services
 ◀ Services

 Thorpe St Michael local services → WC ⛽ ☕ 🍴 i 🛏

 ◀ Thorpe St Michael local services ¹₂

 ◀ RAC 200 yds ☎

 ☎ 2 miles AA ▶

◀ WC ♿

◀ Payphone ☎

Information about area boundaries

 HERTFORDSHIRE
County

ARUN DISTRICT COUNCIL ARUNDEL
Town or village

Haven District Council Welcome to AXTLEY Please drive carefully Twinned with Cedant
Town or village

Other information signs

 ↑↓ Priority over oncoming vehicles
White arrow shows traffic with priority

 Ft | M — 6 — 5 | 1.5 — 4 — 3 | 1 — 2 | 0.5 — 1
Water depth at a ford

 Try your brakes
 Keep in low gear
 Escape lane ahead
Emergency stopping lane ahead

 VEHICLE TESTING STATION
Department of Transport approved vehicle testing centre

MOTORCYCLE TEST CENTRE
Motorcycle test centre

 IN OUT
Private access road or property entrance and exit

 NO ENTRY NO EXIT
Prohibited entry to or exit from private access road or property

Direction and information signs, with test-yourself questions

Primary route ring road

'R' repeater sign indicates that you're driving on a ring road that bypasses a town centre.

1 Where would you find this sign?

Select one answer

a At the approach to a roundabout.

b Where you have right of way.

c At the approach to a railway crossing.

d On a road bypassing a town centre.

Repeater tourist sign

The sign is repeating an earlier direction sign to this tourist attraction.

2 What kind of sign is this?

Select two answers

a A park and ride sign.

b A repeater sign.

c A tourist sign.

d An alternative transport sign.

Distance to parking place ahead

There is a parking place ahead at the distance shown.

3 What does this sign mean?

Select one answer

a Parking allowed on the hard shoulder for the next mile.

b No parking allowed for the next mile.

c Parking place 1 mile ahead.

d Multi-level parking garage one mile ahead.

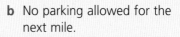

1 d   2 b, c   3 c

Alternative route symbol

One of the symbols that might be used to indicate an alternative route to be followed at a diversion.

4 What does this sign indicate?

Select one answer

a Route for heavy lorries only.

b Hazardous good vehicles only.

c Alternative route.

d Steep uphill then downhill.

Emergency pedestrian exit

Direction to an emergency pedestrian exit in a tunnel.

5 Where would you find this sign?

Select one answer

a In a multi-level parking garage.

b Near a fire escape in a building.

c At a hospital with emergency services.

d In a tunnel.

No through road ahead

There is no through road for vehicles wishing to continue ahead.

The red block indicates the 'dead end'.

6 How would you respond to this sign?

Select one answer

a Look out for overhead structures.

b Expect an airfield runway ahead.

c Do not expect to continue straight ahead.

d Stop at the T-junction ahead.

4 c   5 d   6 c

No through road to the left

There is no through road for vehicles wishing to proceed left.

The red block indicates the 'dead end'.

7 What does this sign mean?

Select one answer

a Emergency stop to the left. ☐

b Accident on motorway slip road. ☐

c Bus terminus to the left. ☐

d No through road to the left. ☐

e Services area to the left. ☐

Priority for oncoming vehicles

The large white arrow indicates which traffic flow has priority.

Give way to traffic having priority.

Where *you* have priority, watch out for oncoming traffic not giving way.

8 What does this sign indicate?

Select one answer

a Oncoming traffic has priority. ☐

b Traffic proceeding ahead has priority. ☐

c Two-way traffic ahead. ☐

d Left lane is wider than right lane. ☐

Road works signs

Road works are temporary situations usually requiring extra caution. Signs specifically for road works normally have black or red information on a yellow background, to ensure maximum visibility.

These signs can be of a warning or regulatory nature, or simply provide information to assist road users.

General response to all road work signs

▶ Approach with caution.

▶ Slow down as necessary.

▶ Obey any regulatory signs, and heed any warnings.

▶ Read all the signs carefully to ensure that you drive in the correct temporary lanes or detours.

▶ Watch out for loose gravel or stones flung up by the tyres of other vehicles.

General signs: advance warning and information

Road works 2 miles ahead   Road works 1 mile ahead   Road works speed limit ¾ mile ahead

Temporary lane layout or diversion signs

▶  Black arrows indicate direction of travel for each lane.

▶ A white arrow indicates an oncoming traffic lane.

▶ A red horizontal line indicates that the lane is closed.

▶ **800 yards**

Distances indicate the distance to where the situation begins.

▶  Speeds shown without a regulatory red circle are the advised maximum speed.

▶ A thin vertical line on the left represents the hard shoulder line.

▶ A thick black vertical line on the right represents the dividing line between carriageways.

▶ Red blocked areas represent road sections not accessible to traffic.

▶ Small inserted regulatory and other signs have their normal meaning for the lane indicated.

▶ Black bend-lines indicate a short temporary traffic diversion.

▶ Signs on a red background are for works vehicles only.

Sometimes a stationary or slow-moving vehicle may have a 'Keep left' sign mounted on the back of the vehicle.

Traffic cones or cylinders mark the edge of temporary lanes or routes.

Barriers indicate where the area is closed to vehicles and pedestrians.

Chevrons indicate a sharp deviation of route, usually where a contra-flow section begins.

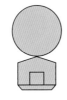 In poor visibility and at night, danger lamps may be used to indicate the edge of a temporary obstruction.

Examples:

Study each of the following road works signs and use the explanations on the previous page to determine what each sign means.

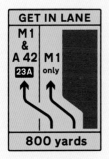

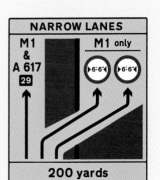

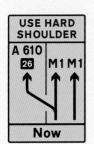

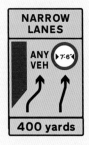

GO   STOP

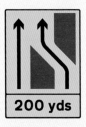

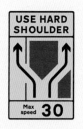

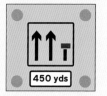

NO HARD
SHOULDER FOR
400 YARDS

SIGN NOT
IN USE

NO ROAD
MARKINGS
FOR
2 MILES

HIGHWAY
MAINTENANCE

Road works signs, with test-yourself questions

Road works information

There are road works for the period shown.

Prepare to slow down and obey any road signs or signals.

Delays are possible, so be patient or choose an alternative route if you need to.

1 How would you interpret this sign?

Select three answers

a Road works ahead for period shown.

b Employment offered at road works ahead.

c Be patient during road works.

d Plan your future journeys accordingly.

Pass to the side indicated

Usually at a road works site.

'Keep left' sign on the back of a stationary or slow-moving vehicle.

Pass to the side indicated by the arrow.

2 How would you respond to this sign on the back of a vehicle?

Select two answers

a Pass to the left, if the vehicle is stationary.

b Take the next exit to the left.

c If you need to overtake, do so to the left of the vehicle.

d Move on to the hard shoulder on the left.

Lanes closed ahead

The two lanes with the red lines are closed ahead at the distance indicated.

If you're in one of those lanes, plan to move safely into the nearside open lane.

If you're in an open lane:

▶ increase your following distance;

▶ allow vehicles from the right to merge into your lane;

▶ look out for vehicles suddenly cutting in front of you.

3 You are in the second lane from the left, travelling behind other vehicles. How should you react when you see this sign?

Select two answers

a Increase your speed to stop vehicles cutting in suddenly from the right-hand lanes. ☐

b Increase your following distance in case vehicles from the right cut in suddenly. ☐

c Allow vehicles from the right to merge into your lane. ☐

d Move to a right-hand lane and go faster. ☐

e Move to the right if you intend turning right at the two T-junctions ahead. ☐

Contra-flow system applies

Stay in your lane even though the right-hand lane moves across to what is normally an oncoming carriageway.

There will be no permanent barrier between you and oncoming traffic.

Don't travel faster than the recommended maximum speed shown.

Keep a safe following distance.

4 You're in the right-hand lane. How must you respond to this sign at a road works situation?

Select one answer

a Move into the left lane at the contra-flow section. ☐

b Stay in your lane at the contra-flow section. ☐

c Swerve to the right to avoid workers. ☐

d Don't cross on to the oncoming carriageway. ☐

ROAD SIGNS, SIGNALS AND MARKINGS

Road markings

Road markings are painted on the surface of the road in white, red or yellow paint. Generally, more dangerous hazards and more important restrictions are emphasized by more prominent markings, such as the use of red paint and broader or more frequent lines. In some situations road markings are complementary to a road sign. The difference in thickness and length of the lines, and the spaces between the parts of a marking, convey the different meanings.

Like road signs, road markings must be obeyed.

Edge lines along the road

Lines along the edge of the main carriageway are used to guide motorists or mark stretches of the road where certain restrictions apply.

Edge line to indicate edge of carriageway

Edge line with raised ribs for roads with hard shoulders

Edge of carriageway at junctions and exits, or between the main carriageway and a lane leaving the main carriageway ahead

Edge of main carriageway at junctions and exits from private drives

Lines along the main carriageway

Lines and other markings on the main carriageway are used to separate lanes of traffic, guide traffic near junctions, warn of hazards ahead and mark stretches of the road where certain restrictions apply, such as no overtaking.

Centre line between traffic moving in opposite directions

Hazard warning line to indicate a potential hazard ahead

Lane line to separate adjacent lanes

Chevron marking to separate traffic flow

Reflective road studs to indicate edges of carriageway

No-crossing line if the solid lane is closest to you

No-crossing line for oncoming vehicles

No-crossing dividing line for vehicles travelling in both directions

Broken boundary lines mean keep clear of hatched markings unless safe to enter the hatched area

Solid boundary lines mean keep clear of hatched markings at all times

Lines across the road

Lines across the road indicate where to stop or give way in accordance with a road sign. Note the difference in thickness and length of the lines, and the spaces between the parts of each painted line. These differences indicate the different meanings of the various line markings.

Stop line at a 'Stop' sign
Stop before the line

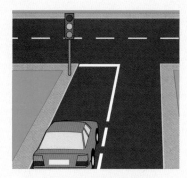

Stop line at traffic signals
Stop before the line

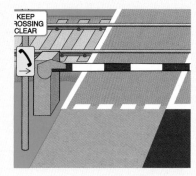

Stop line for pedestrians
at a level crossing

Give way line at a major crossroads
Give way to traffic on the
major road

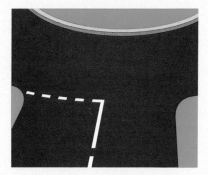

Give way line at a roundabout
Give way to traffic from the right

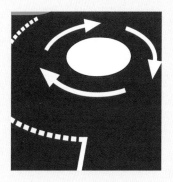

Give way line at a mini-
roundabout
Give way to traffic from the
right

Lines for suitable pedestrian
crossing place at signals or
where controlled by an official

Speed awareness lines
Slow down well ahead of
the junction/roundabout

Rumble bars indicating a
hazard ahead
Slow down and approach
with caution

ROAD SIGNS, SIGNALS AND MARKINGS

Arrows on the road

Various arrows are used to indicate where specific lanes will lead, or to specify a compulsory movement such as a left turn.

Arrows indicate the lanes to use for particular destinations

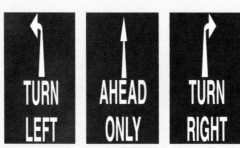

Arrows and words indicating compulsory movement for each lane

Diverge arrows show where traffic streams divide

Deflection arrows indicating which side to pass no-go areas (hatched markings, double white lines, etc.) or to show the route for high vehicles to follow under a low arch bridge

Possible traffic movements at the end of a bus lane

Road humps to control speed. Slow down appropriately

Symbols and words on the road

Words and symbols are often painted on the road surface to give instructions or to prohibit entry.

BUS LANE

Lane reserved for buses

STOP

Stop before the 'Stop' line

Slow down

NO ENTRY

No entry to vehicles

Keep the carriageway clear between the two solid white lines

Marks the limits of a measured distance for police assessment of traffic speed

Markings for reserved or restricted stopping, waiting or parking

Words and markings are often painted on the road surface to prohibit or restrict waiting, parking or loading. Where no times are shown, the restriction applies 24 hours a day.

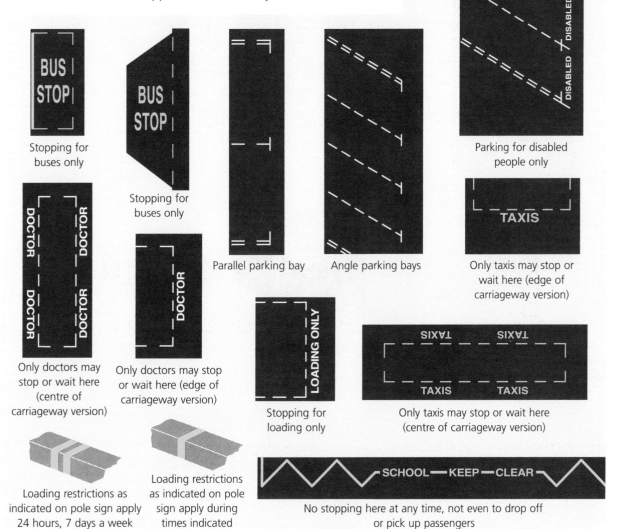

Stopping for buses only

Stopping for buses only

Only doctors may stop or wait here (centre of carriageway version)

Only doctors may stop or wait here (edge of carriageway version)

Parallel parking bay

Angle parking bays

Stopping for loading only

Parking for disabled people only

Only taxis may stop or wait here (edge of carriageway version)

Only taxis may stop or wait here (centre of carriageway version)

Loading restrictions as indicated on pole sign apply 24 hours, 7 days a week

Loading restrictions as indicated on pole sign apply during times indicated

No stopping here at any time, not even to drop off or pick up passengers

Pedestrian crossing markings

Special markings exist to indicate pedestrian crossings, and drivers must strictly obey the rules governed by these markings.

In the area of the zig-zag lines:

▶ Don't park or wait.

▶ Don't overtake the moving vehicle nearest the crossing, or the leading vehicle that has stopped to give way to pedestrians.

▶ When giving way to pedestrians, stop just before the white line across the roadway.

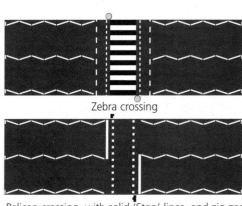

Zebra crossing

Pelican crossing, with solid 'Stop' lines, and zig-zag lines where you may not overtake

Road markings, with test-yourself questions

School – keep clear

Don't stop on these markings at any time, not even to set down or pick up schoolchildren or other passengers.

1 You may not stop on this yellow marking:

Select one answer

a Except when other parking areas are all occupied. ☐

b Except when dropping off schoolchildren. ☐

c At any time at all. ☐

d Except when picking up schoolchildren. ☐

Zig-zag lines

Appear before and after a pedestrian crossing.

Between the start and end of these lines:

▶ Don't park or wait.

▶ Don't overtake the moving vehicle nearest the crossing.

▶ Don't overtake the leading vehicle that has stopped to give way to pedestrians.

▶ When giving way to pedestrians, stop just before the broken white line.

2 What do the zig-zag lines near a pedestrian crossing mean?

Select one answer

a Don't stop on or opposite the lines at any time. ☐

b Don't park on or opposite the lines at any time. ☐

c Don't overtake the moving vehicle nearest the crossing. ☐

d Don't overtake the leading vehicle that has stopped to give way to pedestrians. ☐

e a and b above. ☐

f a, b, c and d above. ☐

Carriageway edge line

Indicates the left-hand edge of the carriageway.

Keep to the right of the line.

3 What does this white line mean?

Select one answer

a Indicates the emergency lane. ☐

b Indicates the edge of the carriageway. ☐

c No left turn allowed. ☐

d Pedal cycle lane. ☐

1 c   2 f   3 b

Centre line

A broken white line with equal-length lines and spaces.

Traffic on each side of the marking is travelling in opposite directions.

Keep to the left of the line. You may cross over if you wish to overtake another vehicle and it is safe to so.

4 **What does this line mean?**

Select two answers

a Centre island line.

b You may cross to overtake if it is safe to do so.

c No overtaking or crossing at any time.

d Centre line on carriageway.

Hazard warning line

Long white lines with short gaps.

Warns of a hazard ahead.

Don't cross to overtake unless the road ahead is clear.

5 **What does this marking mean?**

Select two answers

a Don't cross unless the road ahead is clear.

b Warns of a hazard ahead.

c Centre line to guide traffic flow.

d No overtaking allowed at any time.

No crossing from either side

Appears where overtaking is not safe.

No crossing, except:

▶ for access to or from a side road or property;

▶ to pass a stationary vehicle blocking your lane;

▶ to overtake a pedal cycle, horse or road works vehicle not exceeding 10 mph.

6 **What does this road marking mean?**

Select one answer

a Don't cross the solid white line.

b No overtaking.

c You may cross the line to access property.

d You may cross the line to overtake a slow-moving road works vehicle.

e Oncoming vehicles may not cross the solid white line.

f All of the above.

No crossing line next to centre line

Appears where overtaking is not safe for traffic moving straight ahead.

The no-crossing rule applies only to the traffic having the solid white line closest to it. Other traffic may cross to overtake, if it is safe to do so.

The same exceptions apply as with the double no-crossing line.

7 When may you cross the solid white line to overtake safely?

Select one answer

a When it is on the other side of the centre broken line. ☐

b When it is on my side of the centre broken line. ☐

c Never. ☐

d When the road ahead is clear. ☐

Deflection arrow

Deflection arrows indicate which side to pass no-go areas (hatched markings, double white lines, etc.) or show the route for high vehicles to follow under a low-arched bridge.

8 What does the white arrow mean?

Select one answer

a Left turn ahead. ☐

b Sharp left bend ahead. ☐

c Pull over to the left ahead. ☐

d Keep to the left of the solid white line ahead. ☐

Reflective road studs

Different-coloured studs are used to guide motorists at night or during poor visibility.

The following colours are used to indicate:

○ (white) lane markings or the centre of the road;

▨ (amber) edge of the central reservation (on dual carriageways);

■ (red) left edge of the carriageway;

● (green) entrances to and exits from slip roads and laybys;

● (green) roadworks and contraflow systems.

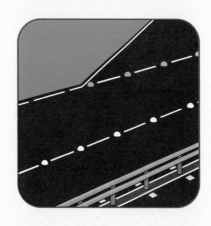

9 What do the red reflective studs indicate?

Select one answer

a No stopping. ☐

b Pedestrians may be on the road. ☐

c Left edge of the carriageway. ☐

d Speed limit applies. ☐

Give way just ahead

Warns that you must give way at the 'Give way' line just ahead.

10 Where would you expect to see this road marking?

Select one answer

a   Where the road is about to divide.

b   Where you must keep left.

c   Just before a 'Give way' line at a junction.

d   At the beach, where ice creams can be bought.

Bus lane

The lane is reserved for use by buses only.

Other vehicles may not drive in that lane.

A broken line indicates that you may drive in the lane only if it is unavoidable.

11 What should the driver of a car do when seeing this marking?

Select one answer

a   Avoid overtaking buses.

b   Give way to pedestrians getting off buses.

c   Stay out of the lane reserved for buses.

d   No response at all.

Pedal cycle lane

The lane is reserved for use by pedal cycles only.

Other vehicles may not drive in that lane.

A broken line indicates that you may drive in the lane only if it is unavoidable.

12 What should the driver of a car do when seeing this marking?

Select one answer

a   Give way to pedal cyclists.

b   Speed up to get past pedal cyclists.

c   No need to do anything.

d   Stay out of the lane reserved for pedal cycles.

Keep clear of entrance

Appears where there are off-street premises or a dropped kerb for pedestrians to cross.

Stationary vehicles must keep clear of the area governed by the marking.

13 What does this marking mean?

Select one answer

a No overtaking.

b No turning left.

c Stationary vehicles must keep clear.

d Marked pedestrian crossing.

Stop line

Appears at junctions requiring vehicles to stop.

Stop just before the white 'Stop' line.

Move off when safe to do so.

14 Where should your vehicle stop at this marking?

Select one answer

a Before the word STOP.

b With your front wheels on the white line across the road.

c Just before the white line across the road.

d Just over the white line so that you can see crossing traffic clearly.

Give way line

Appears at a roundabout.

Wait before the broken line when giving way to traffic from the right.

15 What does this marking mean?

Select one answer

a Stop on the broken line at a traffic light.

b Stop before the broken line when giving way at a roundabout.

c Pedestrian crossing at a roundabout.

d I haven't got a clue!

Speed reduction road hump

Appears where a slower speed is required.

Slow down and drive carefully. Look out for pedestrians on the road.

16 What should you do when you see this marking?

Select one answer

a Keep left because of oncoming traffic.

b Stay in your lane.

c Check your shock absorbers at the next garage.

d Slow down and drive carefully.

Motorway slip road markings

Appears on a motorway slip road.

Don't drive on the marked area except in an emergency.

17 Which statements are correct for this marking?

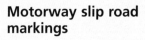

Select two answers

a Indicates two lanes merging.

b Found on a motorway slip road.

c Keep clear of the markings.

d Warns of a road hump ahead.

Speed awareness lines

Appear on the approach to a roundabout or dangerous junction.

They alert you to adjust your speed.

Slow down and look well ahead in good time.

18 How should you respond to these yellow lines?

Select one answer

a Slow down for pedestrians.

b Look out for speed humps ahead.

c Slow down for a roundabout or junction ahead.

d Be careful of schoolchildren crossing between the lines.

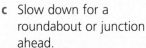

Motorway signs and signals

A motorway is a multi-lane high-speed road. Because traffic travels faster on motorways than on other roads, there is less time to react, so drivers need to be even more observant than usual.

You should look well ahead for road signs and signals so that you are aware of the traffic and road situations ahead, and can plan which lane to use for the next stage of your journey.

Motorway roadside signs

▶ Information signs on motorways are white on a blue background with a white border.

▶ Signs to tourist attractions have a brown background.

▶ A motorway symbol indicates where motorway regulations start to apply.

▶ An arrow with a motorway symbol indicates the direction to a motorway.

▶ Junction numbers are shown on a black background on the main sign.

▶ Before setting off on a journey that includes a motorway, use a road map to check which junction number you need for your exit from the motorway.

▶ When on the motorway, keep an eye on the numbers of the junctions as you pass them, so you will be aware when you are approaching the junction number you need.

▶ About a mile before a junction there is usually a sign that indicates:
– the number of the road leading off the motorway;
– the main destination(s) on that road;
– the junction number, shown on a black background.

▶ Look ahead for the junction number you need so that you can move into the correct lane in good time and leave the motorway safely.

▶ The sign is normally repeated about half a mile before the junction.

▶ Where a second junction follows soon after the first junction, the 1-mile and ½-mile signs may also show information relating to the second junction.

▶ From about 300 yards before the start of the deceleration lane, countdown markers indicate the remaining distance to the point where the lane begins, with each 100 yards represented by a white sloping bar.

▶ At the start of the deceleration lane a sign shows the main destination(s) ahead on the motorway.

▶ Where the deceleration lane separates from the main carriageway there is usually a final route marker.

▸ The sign below indicates that 2 miles further on there is a junction with another motorway.

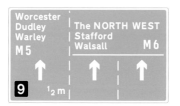

▸ The following ½-mile sign indicates that:
  – there is a reduction in the number of lanes proceeding straight ahead;
  – the left lane leads to another route at the junction ahead.

▸ At the point where the two routes split, a variation of the above sign is usually shown.

▸ No countdown markers are used at this type of junction, because there is no deceleration lane.

▸ After a junction, a route confirmation sign confirms the route you are on, and shows the distances in miles to the main destinations ahead.

▸ Sometimes additional separate signs are used to avoid having too much information on the main signs.

▸ A blue and white map-sign on a slip road leading off a motorway indicates:
  – the road layout ahead;
  – main routes and destinations on a green panel;
  – non-primary routes and destinations on a white panel.

▸ A circular road layout shows that the motorway terminates at a roundabout.

▸ Where a slip road or section behind the hard shoulder is reserved for specific road users only, this is indicated by special signs.

▸ Where there is no hard shoulder across a bridge, a sign will indicate the distance for which this is the case.

▸ On most motorways there are service areas at intervals of roughly half an hour (30 miles), which:
  – are open 24 hours a day, 365 days a year;
  – offer fuel and free parking and toilets;
  – may also provide other services and facilities.

▸ After a motorway junction there is often a sign to indicate the distance to the next motorway service area.

▸ Thereafter, before each service area, there will be a 1-mile advance sign followed by a ½-mile advance sign and a sign at the start of the deceleration lane.

 1 mile ahead

 Half a mile ahead

 At deceleration lane

ROAD SIGNS, SIGNALS AND MARKINGS

Motorway roadside signs continued

▶ At the entrance to a service area or other off-carriageway facility, a sign indicates where the motorway regulations no longer apply.

▶ The end of a motorway, and therefore of motorway regulations, is indicated by this sign:

▶ There is usually an advance sign indicating the distance to where the motorway ends.

Motorway overhead direction signs

▶ Overhead gantry signs are placed above the carriageway on some motorways to alert drivers to junctions ahead.

▶ They are positioned on the same principle as roadside signs:
  – a 1-mile advance sign;
  – a ½-mile advance sign;
  – a sign at the start of the deceleration lane.

▶ The distance to the junction is shown, as well as the junction number.

▶ In the sign combination above:
  – The sloping arrow sign indicates the destinations that can be reached via this exit.
  – The lower sign indicates the destinations that can be reached by continuing on the main carriageway.
  – All lanes may be used to continue straight ahead.
  – The sloping arrow indicates that there is no reduction in the number of lanes.

▶ In the following gantry sign:
  – The left lane will take you to Marlow, and cannot be used if you wish to proceed straight ahead.
  – The two right lanes will take you to the destinations shown, and cannot be used if you wish to go to Marlow.

  – The downward arrows mean *'Decide your destination and get into the correct lane safely and in good time'*.
  – The distance to the junction is shown, as well as the junction number.
  – No countdown markers are used at this kind of junction because there is a reduction in the number of lanes on the main carriageway, and therefore no deceleration lane.

Motorway light signals

Motorway light signals are turned on when it is necessary to tell drivers that they must take particular actions, or to warn of conditions ahead.

▶ Look out for signals ahead, and respond promptly and appropriately.

▶ Signals located on the central reservation or at the back of the hard shoulder apply to all lanes of traffic.

▶ Signals on a gantry over the road apply only to the lane below the particular signal.

▶ Signals consist of two pairs of lights that flash alternately.

Flashing amber lights

▶ Flashing amber lights mean *'Pay attention to the notice displayed.'*

Risk of fog ahead

▶ A vertical row of white lights represents a lane on the carriageway.

▶ A horizontal double row of white lights at the top of a lane row indicates that the lane is closed to traffic.

▶ You may see the following flashing amber signals:

Left lane closed

Centre and right lanes closed

Temporary maximum speed advised

Leave motorway at next junction

(Overhead gantry signal) Move into next lane as indicated

End of restriction

Flashing red lights

▶ Flashing red signals mean Stop!

▶ You may see the following flashing red signals:

Stop, all lanes ahead closed

(Overhead gantry signal) Do not proceed any further in this lane

(At motorway entrance) All lanes are closed. Do not enter the motorway

Signals on older motorways

Hazard ahead. Speed limit 30 mph to beyond the hazard

Motorway signs and signals, with test-yourself questions

End of motorway

The motorway ends ahead at the distance shown.

Motorway rules will no longer apply from that point.

Prepare to reduce speed and adapt to the new traffic situations.

1 What does this sign mean?

Select two answers

a No entry to motorway 1 mile ahead.

b Motorway rules no longer apply 1 mile ahead.

c Don't proceed under low bridge ahead.

d Motorway damaged 1 mile ahead. Take alternative route.

e Motorway ends 1 mile ahead.

Motorway direction sign

On a motorway, indicates junction ahead, with route number and destination.

A white number on a black panel gives the junction number.

2 What does the number in the small black panel mean?

Select one answer

a 25 miles to Nottingham.

b Route 25 is an alternative route to Nottingham.

c It is the number of the next junction.

d Minimum speed allowed on the A52.

Motorway lane closed ahead

'T' lights indicate lanes closed to traffic ahead.

If you see this signal above the lane you're in, prepare to move safely into an open lane.

If you are in an open lane, look out for vehicles wishing to move into your lane, and allow them in safely.

3 What do these signals mean on a motorway?

Select one answer

a No through road ahead.

b Left lane closed ahead.

c Left lane reserved for taxis only.

d Left lane leads to a toll gate.

1 b, e   2 c   3 b

Leave at next junction

Traffic must leave the motorway at the next junction.

Be sure to obey the signal.

4 You see this sign on a motorway. How do you respond?

Select one answer

a Drive carefully round the sharp bend ahead.

b Turn into the one-way street ahead.

c Leave the motorway at the next junction.

d Move into the next lane to your left.

End of restriction

The restriction indicated earlier no longer applies.

5 What does this signal mean?

Select one answer

a This is the end of the motorway.

b The tarred road surface comes to an end.

c The restriction no longer applies.

d End of bus lane on motorway.

Recommended speed limit

Indicates temporary advisable maximum speed on the motorway, possibly because of a hazard ahead.

Don't exceed the speed indicated, as this could be dangerous.

6 What does this overhead signal on a motorway mean?

Select one answer

a Maximum speed allowed in these lanes.

b Minimum speed allowed in these lanes.

c Maximum advisable speed for these lanes.

d Minimum advisable speed for these lanes.

Change lane

Move into the next lane on the side indicated by the arrow.

If this signal is above the lane you're travelling in, don't remain in that lane.

7 How would you react to this overhead motorway signal?

Select one answer

a Pull over to the hard shoulder.

b Move into the next lane on the left.

c Leave the motorway now.

d Check your left-hand tyre pressure.

Stop, all lanes ahead closed

You must stop immediately.

Don't take chances by continuing; there is a dangerous hazard ahead.

8 What does this overhead motorway signal mean?

Select one answer

a Slow down. Bridge ahead.

b Motorway expands to three lanes ahead.

c Stop quickly and safely.

d Slow down but keep moving.

General rules and regulations

When driving on public roads there are specific requirements for various road situations and driving conditions. These requirements are there to protect the rights and lives of all road users.

Basic rules for safe driving

▌ Adapt your driving to the type and condition of the road you are on.

▌ Take into account the road and traffic conditions.

▌ Be prepared for difficult or unexpected situations.

▌ Be prepared to adjust your speed as a precaution.

▌ Periodically look in the mirror and blind spots to see what is happening behind and alongside you.

▌ Look out for pedestrians crossing between vehicles.

▌ Look out for vehicles emerging from junctions.

▌ When manoeuvring, always follow the sequence: Mirrors - Signal - Manoeuvre (M-S-M).

Before moving off

▌ Check in all the mirrors to ensure that the road is clear.

▌ Look over your shoulder to check in the blind spots for pedestrians and traffic.

▌ If the road is clear, signal your intention to move off.

▌ Check in the blind spots again and move off only if there is a safe gap to do so.

Before moving off

You must be able to move off safely and smoothly without creating a dangerous situation for other road users. You will have to perform this manoeuvre on the flat, on an incline and from behind a parked vehicle. The examiner will be watching your use of the controls and your observation in respect of other road users.

Things you must do
▌ Select first gear.

▌ Get clutch control and move off smoothly when it is safe to do so.

Some don'ts
▌ Don't signal without first looking.

▌ Don't move off without first looking.

▌ Don't do anything to make other road users stop or change direction.

▌ Don't accelerate aggressively.

▌ Don't move off in a high gear.

▌ Don't stall the engine or spin the wheels.

Once moving

▌ Drive on the left unless directed to do otherwise by an official, by a road sign or by road surface markings.

▌ You may drive on the right in order to overtake, turn right, or pass parked vehicles or pedestrians.

▌ When approaching a right-hand bend, keep well to the left to improve your view of the road ahead and to avoid colliding with oncoming traffic.

▌ Anticipate the actions of pedestrians and cyclists, and in particular children who may unexpectedly enter the road.

▌ Don't drive in lanes reserved for buses, cycles or trams, unless permitted by a road sign.

▌ Don't drive across a pavement, footpath or bridleway, except to gain lawful access to property.

▌ Anticipate traffic situations early so that you can ease off on the accelerator and time your approach to reduce fuel consumption.

Speed limits

The table to the right shows the national speed limits that apply to all roads unless road signs show otherwise.

▶ Where there are street lights on a road, this generally indicates a speed limit of 30 mph unless there are signs to indicate otherwise.

▶ Some narrow residential streets may have a speed limit of 20 mph.

Traffic-calming zones

▶ Traffic-calming measures are used to slow down traffic in order to make the road safer for vulnerable road users such as pedestrians.

▶ Reduce speed when approaching these road humps, chicanes and narrowings in the road.

▶ Allow cyclists and motorcyclists to pass through traffic-calming measures.

▶ Drive slowly throughout a traffic-calming zone.

▶ If directed by a traffic sign, give way to oncoming traffic.

▶ Don't overtake moving vehicles in a traffic-calming zone.

		Built-up areas	Single carriageway	Dual carriageway	Motorway
		MPH	MPH	MPH	MPH
Cars and motorcycles		30	60	70	70
Cars towing a van or trailer		30	50	60	60
Buses and coaches		30	50	60	70
Goods vehicles up to 7.5 tonnes		30	50	60	70*
Good vehicles over 7.5 tonnes		30	40	50	60

* 60mph if an articulated vehicle, or a vehicle towing a trailer.

Adapting your driving to the weather

Driving in the wet

▶ Tyres grip less well on wet roads, so stopping distance is at least double that for stopping on dry roads.

▶ Increase your following distance substantially to improve your view.

▶ Look out for spray from other vehicles' tyres that will reduce your vision, and pull back further if necessary to improve your view.

▶ To be more visible in spray, switch on your dipped headlights.

▶ If visibility is less than 100 metres (328 feet), switch on your rear fog lights.

▶ Be careful of motorcyclists who may swerve to avoid slippery drain covers and other hazards.

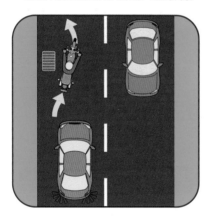

▶ If the vehicle starts to aquaplane – when the tyres lose grip and slide on the water, and the steering becomes light – slow down gradually.

▶ Anti-lock brakes may not always prevent skidding on wet surfaces. (This also applies when driving on dry gravel and shingle surfaces.)

▶ A four-wheel drive improves road-holding on wet roads.

▶ Be careful during rain after a dry spell: surfaces may be slippery, and steering and braking could be affected.

Driving in ice and snow

▶ Don't drive in icy or snowy weather conditions unless it is essential.

▶ If you must drive in such weather, take warm clothing, a warm drink, emergency food and a spade in case of a breakdown.

▶ Remove any snow and ice from all the windows before setting off.

▶ If you need to, stop safely and clear the windows by hand.

▶ Make sure that the lights and number plates are clean.

▶ Clear the mirrors and demist the windows thoroughly.

▶ Stopping distances can be 10 times greater on icy roads than on dry roads.

▶ Increase your following distance substantially.

▶ Drive very carefully, even on gritted roads, and also when overtaking a gritting vehicle, particularly if you are riding a motorcycle.

▶ Don't overtake a snowplough unless the lane you want to use has been cleared.

▶ Expect variable road conditions over short stretches of road.

▶ Don't take sudden actions that could cause skidding.

▶ When moving off in snow, use the highest gear you can.

▶ Drive slowly in a high gear to avoid wheel spin.

▶ If necessary, fit chains to your wheels to help prevent skidding.

▶ Accelerate and brake gently.

▶ Slow down progressively well before a bend and steer smoothly through the bend, avoiding any sudden actions.

▶ If the tyres are almost silent, or your steering feels unresponsive, this may indicate that you are travelling on ice.

▶ Choose a safe place to brake gently in order to check the tyre grip on the road.

Driving in strong winds

▶ Strong wind and sudden gusts can blow high-sided vehicles, cars, cyclists and motorcyclists off course and into your path.

▶ Beware of strong gusts:
  – on open stretches of road;
  – when passing bridges or gaps in hedges, or between buildings;
  – and when passing high-sided vehicles.

▶ Turbulence created by large vehicles may affect your vehicle in windy weather, so increase your following distance.

▶ Look out for motorcyclists overtaking or passing high-sided vehicles.

▶ Take extra care when passing pedal cyclists.

General rules and regulations

The number in brackets at the end of each question indicates how many correct answers you should mark.

1 How can you protect the lives of all road users? (2)

a   Be prepared for difficult situations.

b   Always apply the M-S-M sequence.

c   Hoot before entering a junction.

d   Indicate your intention to proceed.

2 What actions should be performed before moving off? (2)

a   Depress the accelerator to build up power.

b   Engage the handbrake.

c   Look in the rear view mirrors.

d   Look in the relevant blind spot.

3 Under what conditions may you drive on the right side of the road? (3)

a   When instructed to do so by a traffic official.

b   When instructed to do so by a road sign.

c   When driving on a narrow road with a painted barrier island.

d   In order to overtake a slower-moving vehicle.

4 When you approach a right-hand bend in the road, what should you do? (1)

a   Move to the centre of the road.

b   Look out for vehicles parked on the left.

c   Keep well to the left of the road.

d   None of these.

5 Under what conditions may you drive across a bridleway? (1)

a   To take a short cut.

b   In order to test the operation of the brakes.

c   To gain lawful access to property on the other side.

d   All of these.

6 What speed is generally indicated by the presence of street lights? (1)

a   30 mph.

b   20 mph.

c   25 mph.

d   40 mph.

7 How should a driver react in a traffic-calming zone? (1)

a   Give way to cyclists and motorcyclists.

b   Reduce speed.

c   Don't overtake moving vehicles.

d   All of these.

8 Which of the following statements is correct? (1)

a   On wet roads the stopping distance is doubled.

b   If the vehicle starts to aquaplane in wet weather you should reduce speed.

c   Anti-lock brakes may not always prevent skidding on wet roads.

d   All of these.

9 In snowy conditions you should: (1)

a   Not overtake a snow plough.

b   Reduce speed if the tyres become silent.

c   Move off in the highest gear possible.

d   All of these.

10 In snowy conditions you should: (1)

a   Accelerate and brake gently.

b   Increase your following distance substantially.

c   Check the tyre grip on the road in a safe place.

d   All of these.

11 Which of the following should you have in the vehicle in snowy conditions? (1)

a   Warm clothing.

b   Warm drinks.

c   Emergency food.

d   All of these.

12 Which of the following statements is wrong? (1)

a   Strong winds can blow high-sided vehicles into your path.

b   Pedal cyclists are less vulnerable than other traffic in strong winds.

c   Expect strong gusts of wind when passing gaps in hedges.

d   In strong wind, you should increase your following distance behind large vehicles.

12 b	11 d	10 d	9 d	8 d	7 d
6 a	5 c	4 c	3 a, b, d	2 c, d	1 a, b

Driving in fog

▶ If there is fog, allow more time for your journey.

▶ Before setting out in fog, check that your lights are working and make sure that the windows are clean.

▶ Thick fog can occur suddenly in patches and reduce visibility, so look out for fog signals.

▶ Before entering fog, look in the mirrors to check for other road users behind or alongside your vehicle, then slow down if safe to do so.

▶ Switch on your dipped headlights.

▶ Maintain a safe following distance behind the vehicle ahead of you; it may stop suddenly.

▶ Make sure that you can stop safely within the clearly visible space ahead, and reduce speed if necessary.

▶ Switch on your windscreen wipers and demisters.

▶ Look out for other vehicles not using headlights.

▶ Don't use front and rear fog lights unless visibility is seriously reduced, to less than 100 metres (328 feet), because they dazzle other road users and obscure your brake lights.

▶ Where visibility is poor at a junction, stop in the correct position, and listen carefully for other traffic before moving off.

▶ Once you've moved off, move through the junction safely and don't block approaching cross-traffic.

▶ If there is a vehicle close behind you, use your brake lights to indicate that you are slowing down to increase the gap in front of you. (Don't accelerate to try to increase the gap behind you.)

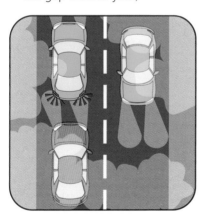

▶ Switch off the fog lights immediately visibility improves sufficiently.

Driving in hot conditions

▶ Open your window for fresh air to avoid drowsiness.

▶ Be careful of soft tarmac surfaces caused by hot weather as this could affect steering and braking.

Waiting and parking

▶ To park in a space reserved for the disabled, you must display a recognized orange or blue badge on the bottom left-hand corner of the windscreen.

▶ Where restriction periods are displayed on upright signs, don't wait or park on:
  – yellow lines along the edge of a carriageway;
  – school entrance markings on a carriageway.

▶ Wherever possible, park in off-street parking areas or parking bays marked on the road with white lines.

▶ When stopping on the roadside:
  – Stop as close as you can to the side.
  – Ensure that passengers get out on the kerb side of the vehicle.

  – Don't stop too close to a vehicle displaying an orange 'disabled' badge.
  – Ensure that your vehicle is locked when you leave.

▶ When parking on the roadside:
  – Switch off the engine, headlights and fog lights.
  – Apply the handbrake before leaving the vehicle.
  – Check before opening the door to ensure that you don't hit anyone.

Waiting and parking

Safe place to stop

The examiner will be watching how you use the M-S-M routine, and your judgement in selecting a safe place to stop.

Things you must do

▶ Use the M-S-M routine.

▶ Select a safe place to stop where you won't obstruct the road or create a hazard.

▶ Stop close to the edge of the road.

Some don'ts

▶ Don't stop without sufficient warning to other road users.

▶ Don't cause a danger or inconvenience to other road users.

No-stopping and no-parking areas

Do not stop or park:

▶ on the carriageway, except in an emergency;

▶ on the hard shoulder of a motorway, except in an emergency;

▶ on a pedestrian crossing, including within the area marked by zig-zag lines;

▶ on a clearway;

▶ on a bus stop clearway during the hours of operation;

▶ on an urban clearway during the hours of operation, except to pick up and set down passengers;

▶ on a road with double white line markings, except to pick up or set down passengers;

▶ on a lane reserved for buses, trams or cycles, when the reservation applies;

▶ on a cycle track;

▶ on red lines on red routes, unless otherwise indicated by a sign;

▶ in such a position that other vehicles would have to enter a tram lane;

▶ in controlled parking areas when waiting restrictions are in force;

▶ in parking spaces reserved for specific users (e.g. orange-badge holders, residents), unless entitled to do so;

▶ where it would endanger, inconvenience or obstruct pedestrians or other road users, for example:
  – near a school entrance;

  – where you would block access for emergency services;
  – at or near a bus stop;
  – at or near a taxi rank;
  – on the approach to a level crossing;

  – opposite or within 10 metres of a junction, unless in a designated parking space;
  – near the crest of a hill;
  – on a hump bridge;
  – opposite a traffic island;
  – opposite a parked vehicle in a narrow road;
  – where the kerb has been lowered for wheelchairs;
  – in front of a property entrance;
  – on a bend;
  – on or partially on a pavement, unless authorized by a sign, as this would obstruct pedestrians, people in wheelchairs, the visually impaired and people with prams or pushchairs.

Parking in fog

▶ If possible, don't park on the road in fog.

▶ Parking lights or sidelights must be switched on if parking in fog is unavoidable.

Parking of goods vehicles

▶ A goods vehicle with a maximum laden weight of over 7.5 tonnes, including trailer, must not park on a verge or pavement or the area between carriageways without police permission – except where this is essential for loading or offloading; the vehicle must not be left unattended.

▶ Don't load or unload at yellow markings on the kerb. Upright signs show any time restrictions that apply.

▶ On red routes there are marked and signed bays to indicate when and where you may load and unload.

Parking at night

▶ Unless in a designated parking space, don't park facing oncoming traffic.

▶ You may park on the right-hand side of a one-way street at night.

▶ Where the speed limit is more than 30 mph, you must have your parking lights on when parked on the road or in a layby on the road.

▶ Where the speed limit is 30 mph or less, all vehicles not exceeding 1,525 kg unladen, invalid carriages and motorcycles may be parked on the road at night without lights, provided they are:
  – at least 10 metres (32 feet) from any junction; and
  – close to the kerb; and
  – facing the direction of the traffic flow; or
  – in a recognized parking place or layby.

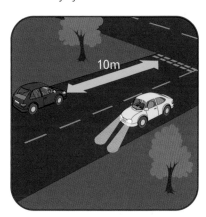

▶ Other vehicles and trailers, and vehicles with projecting loads, must display parking lights if left on the road at night.

Parking on hills

▶ Park close to the kerb and apply the handbrake firmly.

▶ When facing uphill, engage first gear and turn the steering wheel away from the kerb.

▶ When facing downhill, engage reverse gear and turn the steering wheel towards the kerb.

▶ If your vehicle has an automatic gearbox, select 'Park'.

Reverse parking

You will be required to reverse park your car either at the kerb or off the road into a parking bay, without mounting the kerb.

Parking at the kerb

▶ Position your vehicle alongside any parked vehicle.

▶ Look in the mirrors and blind spot to ensure that it is safe to reverse.

▶ If it is safe to do so, select reverse gear and indicate your intention.

▶ Reverse into the space.

▶ Stop reasonably close and parallel to the kerb.

Reversing into a parking bay

▶ Make sure that your vehicle will easily fit into the space.

▶ Look in the mirrors and blind spot to ensure that it is safe to reverse.

▶ If it is safe to do so, signal your intention and reverse into the parking bay.

▶ Stop with the front wheels straight when the vehicle is neatly in the parking bay.

Some don'ts

▶ Don't park too close to any vehicles or road markings.

▶ Don't mount the kerb.

▶ Don't swing from side to side.

▶ Don't park at an angle.

▶ Don't be inconsiderate to other road users.

▶ Don't take too long to complete the manoeuvre.

▶ Don't turn the steering wheel when the vehicle is stationary.

General rules and regulations continued

The number in brackets at the end of each question indicates how many correct answers you should mark.

13 Which of the following should you do in the event of fog? (1)

a Allow more time for the journey.

b Make sure that the windows are clean.

c Look in the mirrors before entering the fog.

d All of these.

14 Which of the following lights should be used when driving in fog? (1)

a Hazard warning lights.

b Main beam headlights.

c Dipped headlights.

d None of these.

15 When driving in fog, if there is a vehicle too close behind you should: (1)

a Use your brake lights to indicate your presence.

b Increase speed slightly.

c Switch on the hazard warning lights.

d None of these.

16 When should you use front and rear fog lights? (1)

a When fog is present.

b When visibility is restricted to less than 100 metres.

c Only in conjunction with hazard warning indicators.

d In the event of an emergency to warn other road users.

17 Which of the following apply in respect of parking? (2)

a Ensure that passengers get out on the kerb side of the vehicle.

b Don't park on school entrance markings.

c Switch on the dipped headlights when parking at night.

d To park in a space reserved for the disabled, you must display a green badge.

18 Which of the following are 'No stopping' areas? (3)

a A clearway.

b A pedestrian crossing.

c A lane reserved for buses.

d A parking bay.

19 Which of the following applies when parking? (1)

a You may park on red lines on red routes.

b Do not park in a manner that forces other traffic to drive in tram lanes.

c You may park on a cycle track.

d You may park for a short period on a taxi rank.

20 Which of the following places is a 'No stopping' area? (1)

a Near the crest of a hill.

b Within 10 metres of a junction.

c Opposite a traffic island.

d All of these.

21 Which of the following applies to the parking of goods vehicles? (1)

a Goods vehicles may load and unload at yellow markings on the kerb.

b Laden goods vehicles over 7.5 tonnes should not park on the verge.

c Goods vehicles should park facing oncoming traffic at night.

d There are marked bays reserved for parking goods vehicles on orange routes.

22 When parking at night, which of the following apply? (2)

a You may park on the right-hand side of a one-way street.

b Where the speed limit is more than 30 mph you must display parking lights.

c Motorcycles without lights should be parked facing oncoming traffic.

d Invalid carriages must have lights.

23 When parking on a hill, you should: (1)

a Park close to the kerb.

b If facing downhill, turn the steering wheel to the kerb.

c If facing uphill, turn the steering wheel away from the kerb.

d All of these.

24 Where the speed limit is 30 mph or less, which of the following applies? (1)

a Vehicles not exceeding 1,525 kg unladen may park without lights at night.

b On red routes there are parking bays marked in blue for the disabled.

c Disabled drivers must display yellow badges to park at night.

d Select 'N' if the vehicle has an automatic gearbox when parking.

13	d	14	c	15	a	16	b
17	a, b	18	a, b, c	19	b	20	d
21	b	22	a, b	23	d	24	a

Traffic lanes

Changing lanes

▶ Before changing lane, look in the mirrors and check the blind spots to make sure it is safe to do so (M-S-M).

▶ When changing lanes, do not cause another road user to swerve or slow down.

▶ If it is safe to change lane, indicate your intention and move across safely.

▶ Obey all road markings and traffic signs when changing lanes.

▶ Don't change lanes suddenly or unnecessarily.

Lane use

▶ On a single carriageway with three lanes and no priority for traffic in either direction:
  – Don't drive in the right-hand lane.
  – Use the middle lane only for turning right or overtaking.

▶ On a single carriageway with four or more lanes:
  – Drive only in the lanes permitted by traffic signs or markings.

▶ On a dual carriageway with two lanes:
  – Drive in the left-hand lane.
  – Drive in the right-hand lane only for turning right and overtaking, and return to the left-hand lane when safe to do so.

▶ On a dual carriageway with three lanes:
  – Drive in the left-hand lane.
  – Drive in the middle lane or right lane for overtaking, but return to the left lane when it is safe to do so.

▶ On a steep hill:
  – Use the climbing or crawler lane if you are driving a slow-moving vehicle, or when other vehicles wish to overtake.

Lane restrictions

▶ Don't drive or park on a cycle lane.

▶ Don't drive or stop in a tram or bus lane during its period of operation.

🚗 Changing lanes

Positioning and lane discipline

Things you must do

▶ Use the M-S-M routine before changing lanes.

▶ Keep to the left when turning left.

▶ Keep to the right when turning right.

▶ Keep clear of parked vehicles.

▶ Move into the correct lane in good time, even where there are no lane markings.

▶ Obey all road signs and markings.

▶ Look out for left- and right-turn arrows at junctions.

▶ Look out for bus and cycle lanes.

Some don'ts

▶ Don't weave from lane to lane.

▶ Don't drive too close to the kerb.

▶ Don't drive unnecessarily in the centre of the road.

▶ Don't change lanes at the last moment or suddenly.

▶ Don't straddle the lane lines.

▶ Don't cut across the path of other traffic when changing lanes in roundabouts.

One-way streets

- General traffic must travel in the direction shown by road signs or markings.
- Buses and cycles may travel in the opposite direction where this is permitted.
- When leaving a one-way street, select the correct lane as soon as possible.
- Do not change lanes suddenly.
- Unless otherwise indicated:
  – Use the left lane if turning left.
  – Use the right lane if turning right.

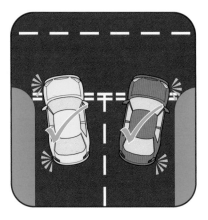

  – If proceeding straight ahead, drive in the appropriate lane.

Country roads

- Slow down when approaching bends, minor junctions and turns that may be partially concealed.
- Be careful of tractors, horse-riders and cyclists on the road ahead; slow down and leave plenty of room as you pass them.
- Reduce speed where country roads enter villages.

- Look out for pedestrians walking towards you on your side of the road; slow down and leave plenty of room as you pass them.

- On narrow, single-track roads use passing places correctly:
  – Pull into a passing place on your left, or wait opposite a passing place on your right, to allow vehicles from behind to overtake you, or oncoming vehicles to pass.
  – Give way to vehicles coming uphill where possible.
  – Be prepared to reverse to the nearest passing place so that oncoming vehicles can pass.
  – Don't park in passing places.

Built-up areas

- On narrow residential streets there may be a maximum speed limit of 20 mph. Look out for:
  – vehicles entering the road from side roads;
  – vehicles moving off from the side of the road;
  – people opening car doors;
  – pedestrians;
  – children playing and entering the road from between parked vehicles;
  – cyclists and motorcycles.

- Beware at junctions where your view of the road ahead may be restricted.

Overtaking

Before overtaking

▶ Make sure that the road ahead is clear for overtaking.

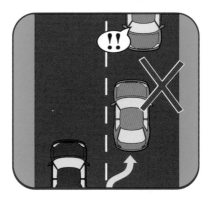

▶ Allow a safe space in front of your vehicle to prepare to overtake.

▶ Ensure that you are not being overtaken by a vehicle behind you.

 Overtaking

The examiner will be watching how safely you overtake in accordance with safe driving requirements.

Things you must do

▶ Allow enough room to pass.

▶ Allow enough space after overtaking.

▶ Look out for oncoming vehicles.

▶ Use the M-S-M routine.

▶ Overtake only if it is safe to do so.

▶ React to road conditions.

▶ Use the controls accordingly.

Some don'ts

▶ Don't overtake if your view of the road ahead is not clear.

▶ Don't overtake if you have to exceed the speed limit to do so.

▶ Don't overtake if the road is narrow.

When overtaking

▶ Overtake only when it is safe to do so.

▶ Don't get too close to the vehicle you wish to overtake.

▶ Check in the mirrors to ensure that it is safe to overtake.

▶ If it is safe to overtake, signal your intention to do so before moving across to overtake.

▶ Look over your shoulder to check in the blind spot, and start to overtake only if it is safe to do so.

▶ Look out for cyclists, horse-riders and motorcyclists, who are more difficult to see.

▶ Allow plenty of space when overtaking, particularly if you are driving a long vehicle or towing a trailer.

▶ Don't follow a vehicle overtaking another vehicle. It is not safe for two vehicles to overtake the same vehicle at the same time.

▶ Move quickly past the vehicle you are overtaking.

▶ Don't pass too close to the other vehicle.

▶ Don't change lanes to the left in order to overtake.

▶ Make sure you are safely clear of the other vehicle before returning to the left-hand side of the road.

▶ Take extra care at night and in poor visibility.

▶ Before passing a parked vehicle or obstruction on your side of the road, give way to oncoming traffic if necessary.

General rules and regulations continued

The number in brackets at the end of each question indicates how many correct answers you should mark.

25 When driving in traffic, if you want to change lanes you should: (2)

a Look in the rear view mirrors to see if it is safe to do so.

b Indicate and move over quickly.

c Look in the blind spots for hidden vehicles.

d Swerve into the correct lane if it is safe to do so.

26 When changing lanes, which of the following must you do? (1)

a Obey all road markings and traffic signs.

b Don't change lanes unnecessarily.

c Use the middle lane only for overtaking.

d All of these.

27 Which of the following applies on a dual carriageway with two lanes? (2)

a Use the right-hand lane only when turning right or overtaking.

b Switch on the parking lights at sunset.

c Drive in the left-hand lane.

d Use the hazard warning lights when fog is present.

28 Which of the following statements are correct when driving in traffic? (2)

a If it is safe to do so, you can change lanes suddenly.

b You may park in an unused cycle lane.

c You should not drive in a bus lane during its period of operation.

d You must drive in the lanes indicated by traffic signs.

29 Which of the following statements are true? (2)

a Buses and cycles may be permitted to travel in the opposite direction in a one-way street.

b In a one-way street you may change lanes without indicating.

c Before turning right from a one-way street you should move to the left of the road.

d In a one-way street, you must select the appropriate lane if proceeding straight ahead.

30 What may the speed limit be in narrow residential streets? (1)

a 15 mph.

b 20 mph.

c 25 mph.

d 30 mph.

31 When driving in a built-up residential area, which of the following may be a hazard? (1)

a Children suddenly entering the road.

b People opening car doors.

c Cyclists moving off from the side of the road.

d All of these.

32 When driving along a country road, which of the following apply? (3)

a Reduce speed when approaching a bend in the road.

b Look out for horse-riders.

c Indicate your intention only when turning right.

d Reduce speed as you enter a village.

33 On a narrow, single-track country lane you must: (1)

a Pull into a passing place to allow vehicles to overtake.

b Give way to vehicles coming uphill.

c Be prepared to reverse to a passing place to allow approaching vehicles to pass.

d All of these.

34 If you wish to overtake a vehicle travelling ahead of you, you must: (1)

a Ensure that the road ahead is clear.

b Create a safe space ahead of your vehicle so that you can overtake.

c Check in the rear view mirrors.

d All of these.

35 What is the last thing you must do before pulling out to overtake? (1)

a Look in the blind spot.

b Indicate your intention.

c Look in the mirror.

d Increase your speed.

36 Which of the following are hazards when overtaking? (3)

a Goods vehicles towing long trailers.

b Horse-riders on the side of the road.

c Poor visibility at night.

d None of these.

25 a, c	26 d	27 a, c
28 c, d	29 a, d	30 b
31 d	32 a, b, d	33 d
34 d	35 a	36 a, b, c

PART FOUR

Overtaking on the left

You may overtake on the left only:

▶ if the vehicle ahead is signalling to turn right, and there is room to do so;

▶ if you are moving in a queue that is faster than the queue on your right; or

▶ if you are in a one-way street.

Overtaking large vehicles

▶ Because lorries are longer than cars it is more difficult and risky to overtake them.

▶ Increase your following distance so that you can see the road ahead and the driver can see you in the mirrors.

▶ Before starting to overtake, make sure there is a safe space ahead to complete the manoeuvre.

▶ Don't follow a vehicle overtaking another vehicle. It is not safe for two vehicles to overtake the same vehicle at the same time.

Where not to overtake

Don't overtake:

▶ if there is any doubt about whether it is safe to do so;

▶ when approaching:
 – a corner or bend;

 – a hump bridge;
 – the brow of a hill;
 – a road junction on the left or right;
 – a school-crossing patrol;

▶ just before turning left;

▶ where the road narrows;

▶ where the view ahead is blocked;

▶ between the kerb and a stationary bus or tram;

▶ where traffic is queuing at junctions or road works;

▶ at a level crossing;

▶ if you have to cross or straddle a 'No overtaking' solid white line;

▶ if you have to cross a solid white line dividing traffic flow;

▶ the nearest moving vehicle to a pedestrian crossing;

▶ a vehicle that has stopped at a pedestrian crossing;

▶ if you have to enter a lane reserved for buses, trams or cycles during reservation times;

▶ if it is prohibited by a 'No overtaking' sign or road marking;

▶ if it would cause another vehicle to slow down or swerve;

▶ a vehicle that is signalling to turn right.

Being overtaken

▶ Keep as far to the left as possible.

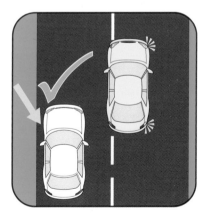

▶ Don't accelerate while being overtaken.

▶ Slow down if necessary to allow the overtaking vehicle to pass.

▶ Drop back to maintain a two-second gap behind the vehicle that has overtaken you.

▶ Don't obstruct vehicles wishing to overtake you, even if you are travelling at the maximum speed allowed.

▶ Check in the mirrors often, and if you are holding up traffic behind you, move to the left where it is safe to allow the traffic to pass.

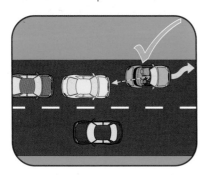

Meeting and passing other vehicles

The examiner will be watching whether you deal with on-coming traffic safely and confidently, including on narrow roads and where there are parked cars or other obstructions.

Things you must do

▶ Use the M-S-M routine.

▶ Give way to oncoming traffic.

▶ Keep well back of any obstruction if you need to stop, to improve your view of the road ahead.

▶ Look out for pedestrians stepping out between parked vehicles.

▶ Look out for vehicles moving off without warning.

▶ React to road conditions.

▶ Use the controls accordingly.

Junctions and turns

▶ Look out for vehicles entering the road at a junction ahead. If necessary, slow down and prepare to stop.

▶ At a junction, when you realize you are in the wrong lane, continue in that lane through the junction, and find somewhere safe to turn.

▶ Look out for pedestrians, cyclists, motorcyclists and horse-riders, who are often more difficult to see.

▶ Be careful at unmarked junctions where no one has priority in side roads and country lanes.

▶ When turning into a road, give way to pedestrians crossing that road, as they have priority.

▶ Look out for long vehicles that need extra road width to turn, and if necessary slow down and allow them to turn.

▶ Don't enter a junction unless there is a clear space on the other side large enough for your vehicle.

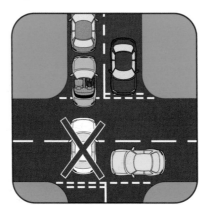

▶ Don't assume that a vehicle entering a junction will turn in the direction in which it is signalling.

▶ Stop or give way in accordance with any road sign, traffic signal or road marking.

▶ In slow-moving traffic, allow access to vehicles moving into and from side roads.

▶ Give way to any vehicle blocking the junction and allow it to get clear.

▶ If your view of the junction is restricted, stop, then move forward slowly until you have an unrestricted view.

▶ When crossing or turning right on a dual carriageway, make sure that the central reservation has enough space for the length of your vehicle.
  – Cross the first half if it is safe to do so.
  – Stop and wait in the central reservation.
  – Enter the second half of the road when it is safe to do so.

▶ Where the central reservation on a dual carriageway is too short for your vehicle, cross only when both carriageways are clear.

Junctions and turns *continued*

▶ At a box junction with criss-cross yellow painted lines:
  – Don't enter the junction when continuing straight ahead, unless there is a clear space on the other side.
  – You may wait on the painted lines if prevented by other traffic from turning right.

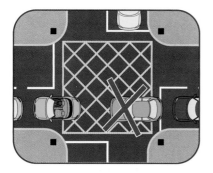

🚗 Junctions and turns

Crossing the path of other vehicles

The examiner will be watching your ability to cross the path of other vehicles safely and confidently. This would include when turning right into a side road or driveway.

Things you must do

▶ Use the M-S-M routine.
▶ Position your vehicle correctly and adjust your speed.
▶ Keep as close to the centre of the road as is safe when turning right.
▶ Give way to oncoming traffic and stop if necessary.
▶ Look out for pedestrians.

Some don'ts

▶ Don't cause other vehicles to slow down, swerve or stop.
▶ Don't cut the corner.
▶ Don't turn too wide beyond the turning point.

Junctions and roundabouts

The examiner will be observing how safely you deal with junctions and roundabouts, including observation, correct positioning of your vehicle, adjusting your speed and using the correct lane.

Things you must do

▶ Use the M-S-M routine.
▶ Stop if necessary.
▶ Use the correct lane for turning.
▶ Maintain an appropriate position and speed on approach.
▶ Observe and judge the situation well.

Some don'ts

▶ Don't approach the junction at the wrong speed.
▶ Don't position and turn incorrectly.
▶ Don't enter the junction dangerously.
▶ Don't stop or wait unnecessarily.

Turning right

▶ Before turning right, look in the mirrors and blind spot for overtaking vehicles and to ensure that it is safe to turn.
▶ Indicate in good time your intention to turn right.
▶ Keep as far to the right of your half of the road as possible, so that vehicles can pass safely on your left.

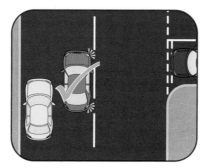

▶ Wait until there is a safe gap in oncoming traffic before commencing the turn, and cross the centre line of the cross road before turning.

▶ Look out for pedestrians, cyclists and motorcyclists.
▶ Check the mirrors and blind spot again to make sure you are not being overtaken, then turn.
▶ Don't cut the corner when turning.
▶ On a one-way road, move into the right-hand lane well before turning.
▶ Where there is an oncoming vehicle also turning right, it is safest to pass the vehicle and turn right behind it (right side to right side).

▶ You may turn across in front of each other, left side to left side, but take extra care.
▶ Road layout/markings could indicate which method to use.

General rules and regulations continued

The number in brackets at the end of each question indicates how many correct answers you should mark.

37 When may you overtake on the left? (1)

a If the vehicle ahead is turning right and there is room to overtake.

b If the lane you are in is moving faster than the lane on your right.

c If you are travelling in a one-way street.

d All of these.

38 Before overtaking a vehicle on a narrow road: (2)

a Increase your following distance to improve your view of the road ahead.

b Ensure that there is a safe space ahead of the vehicle.

c Flash your lights to warn the driver of your intention.

d Follow another vehicle that is already overtaking it.

39 When would it not be safe to overtake another vehicle? (1)

a If you are approaching a bend in the road.

b Just before you intend turning left.

c At a level crossing.

d All of these.

40 When overtaking: (1)

a You may cross a solid white line in order to overtake a hearse.

b You should not overtake if it will cause another vehicle to slow down.

c You may overtake as you approach a junction.

d Overtaking is only prohibited if there is a 'No overtaking' traffic sign.

41 When being overtaken: (2)

a Move to the left of the road.

b Increase the distance behind the vehicle ahead.

c Increase speed slightly.

d Flash the left indicator to signal that it is safe to overtake you.

42 If you are in the wrong lane at a junction: (1)

a Indicate your intention to change lanes.

b Check in the blind spot and, if it is safe to do so, move into the correct lane.

c Stay in the lane and find a suitable place to turn after the junction.

d Allow the traffic behind to pass, then move into the correct lane.

43 When waiting to turn into a junction: (3)

a Give way to pedestrians crossing the road you are entering.

b Make space for long vehicles turning into the road that you are on.

c Give way in accordance with any road signs or markings.

d Rev the engine to encourage pedestrians to cross quickly.

44 When crossing a dual carriageway: (1)

a Cross to the central reservation if it is safe to do so.

b Stop and wait in the central reservation.

c Enter the second half of the road only if it is safe to do so.

d All of these.

45 At a box junction: (2)

a Do not enter the junction unless there is a clear space on the other side.

b Never stop on the yellow-painted area.

c Wait on the painted area if prevented from turning right by another vehicle.

d Use the space to conduct the normal safety observations.

46 When you are about to turn right, what should you do? (1)

a Look in the mirrors and blind spot to the right.

b Engage the 'left turn' indicator.

c Move to the left of the road to give yourself enough space to turn.

d All of these.

47 When turning right: (2)

a Pass any oncoming vehicle and turn right behind it.

b Turn right in front of the vehicle, if it is safe to do so.

c Proceed straight ahead and turn at the next junction.

d Wait for the other vehicle to complete the turn.

48 Which of these applies when about to turn right? (1)

a Use the M-S-M sequence.

b Indicate your intention.

c Look in the mirrors and blind spots before changing direction.

d All of these.

43	a, b, c	44	d	45	a, c	46	a	47	a, b	48	d
37	d	38	a, b	39	d	40	b	41	a, b	42	c

Turning left

▶ Don't overtake just before turning left.

▶ Check in the mirrors to make sure it is safe behind you.

▶ Signal in good time your intention to turn left.

▶ Look over your left shoulder for traffic approaching from behind.

▶ Look out for cyclists and motorcycles on your left.

▶ Keep as close to the left as is safe to do so.

▶ Give way to any vehicles in a reserved lane or tramway.

U-turns

▶ Don't make a U-turn in a busy street. Find a quiet street to turn around.

▶ Look over your shoulder for a final check before making a U-turn.

▶ Make sure that the road is clear in both directions and that it is wide enough to turn safely.

 ## Turning in the road

You will be instructed to drive to a particular area and asked to complete a turn in the road. The vehicle must end up facing in the opposite direction on the left-hand side of the road, and this will take at least three moves.

Things you must do

▶ Check in the mirrors and blind spots to ensure that the road is clear in both directions.

▶ If it is safe to do so, drive forward in first gear and turn the steering wheel as far to the right as possible.

▶ Stop as you approach the far-side kerb, turning the steering wheel as far to the left as you can.

▶ Check in the mirrors and blind spots to ensure that it is safe to continue.

▶ If it is safe to continue, reverse slowly while turning the steering wheel further to the left if possible.

▶ Stop as you approach the far-side kerb, turning the steering wheel as far to the right as you can.

▶ Check in the mirrors and blind spots to ensure that it is safe to continue.

▶ If it is safe to do so, pull forward and position the vehicle alongside the kerb on the opposite side of the road from where you started the turn.

Some don'ts

▶ Don't mount the kerb.

▶ Don't be inconsiderate towards other road users.

▶ Don't take longer than is necessary to complete the manoeuvre.

▶ Don't turn the steering wheel when the vehicle is stationary.

Roundabouts

Approaching a roundabout

▶ Obey all traffic signs, signals and road markings.

▶ Apply the Mirrors - Signal - Manoeuvre (M-S-M) procedure at each stage.

▶ Decide which exit you intend to take, and indicate your intentions in good time.

▶ Move into the correct lane, and adjust your speed accordingly.

▶ Take note of the movements of other vehicles in the roundabout, and look out for vehicles and cyclists not indicating.

At a roundabout entrance

▶ Give way to traffic approaching from the right, unless otherwise directed by a traffic sign, road marking or traffic light.

▶ Obey all traffic signs and markings but be wary of traffic from the right.

▶ Look out for vehicles already on the roundabout, particularly vehicles that may not be signalling.

▶ If you have stopped, make sure there is a clear space in front of you before you enter the roundabout.

On a roundabout

If taking the first exit:

▶ Signal left and move into the left-hand lane.

▶ Keep left and keep signalling to turn left.

If taking an intermediate exit:

▶ Indicate your intention and move into the appropriate lane.

▶ Stay in this lane until you need to exit left.

▶ After passing the exit just before the one you need, indicate your intention to turn left.

When taking the last exit, or passing all exits:

▶ Signal right and move into the right-hand lane.

▶ Stay in the right-hand lane.

▶ After passing the exit just before the one you need, indicate your intention to turn left.

Where there are more than three lanes on the approach road:

▶ Drive in the appropriate lane on approach and through the roundabout.

Be careful of, and give way to:

▶ pedestrians crossing the road;

▶ traffic already on the roundabout, particularly vehicles signalling to leave at the next exit;

▶ traffic straddling the lanes;

▶ vehicles in the wrong lane wishing to turn left;

▶ motorcyclists;

▶ cyclists and horse-riders in the left lane signalling right to indicate that they intend to remain on the roundabout;

▶ long vehicles requiring more width because of their length.

Mini-roundabouts

▶ Approach these as you would normal roundabouts.

▶ Don't drive over the central markings, unless you are driving a large vehicle.

▶ Look out for vehicles making U-turns.

Multiple roundabouts

At some intersections there may be a series of mini-roundabouts.

- Treat each mini-roundabout separately.
- Follow the roundabout rules.

Railway crossings

Basic rules for railway crossings

Most crossings have a steady amber light, twin flashing red 'Stop' lights, and an audible alarm. There may also be full, half- or no barriers.

- Approach and cross the railway line(s) carefully.
- Don't drive too close to the vehicle ahead of you.
- Cross only if there is enough space for your vehicle on the other side.
- Don't stop or park on or near a railway crossing.
- At open crossings with a 'Give way' sign but no gates, barriers, attendants or traffic lights, look in both directions, listen, and cross only if you are sure there is no train approaching.
- Always stop when the traffic light signals show.

- A steady amber light is the first warning that a train is approaching.
- Where there is more than one railway line, look out for this flashing red light signal and a change in the tone of the audible sound to warn that another train is approaching.

Controlled railway crossings

- Stop when the steady amber light is on, if safe to do so.

- If you have already crossed the white line when the amber light comes on, continue to cross the railway line without delay.

- Stop when the red lights are flashing alternately.

- Stop behind the solid white line across the road.

- Remain stationary if the red light continues flashing after a train has passed, because this means another train is about to pass by.
- After stopping, proceed only once the lights have gone off and the barriers have opened.
- Phone the signalman where either:
  - the red light continues flashing and no train passes for more than three minutes, or
  - a half-barrier is lowered but no lights are flashing.
- Stop when a barrier or a half-barrier is being lowered, as this means a train is coming.
- Don't zig-zag around half-barriers.

Controlled railway crossings continued

▶ Where there are no barriers, stop when the warning lights are displayed.

▶ If you are driving a large or slow-moving vehicle, or herding animals, park where instructed to by a sign, and use the railway telephone to obtain permission to cross. Telephone again when you are clear of the crossing.

Drivers of LARGE or SLOW VEHICLES must phone and get permission to cross

LARGE means over 55′ long or 9′6″ wide or 38 tonnes total weight SLOW means 5 mph or less

▶ A flashing red pedestrian light means that pedestrians must stop at the 'Stop' line.

Railway crossings without lights

▶ Stop when the barrier or gate begins to lower, and wait.

▶ Proceed only when the barrier or gate opens.

User-operated railway gates or barriers

These are crossings that have a 'Stop' sign and small red and green lights.

▶ Stop when the red light is on.

▶ Cross only when the green light is on and it is safe to do so.

▶ To cross with a vehicle, open the gates or barriers on both sides of the crossing.

▶ Check that the green light is still on, then cross quickly.

▶ Once clear of the crossing, close the gates or barriers on both sides again.

▶ If there are no lights, but there is a telephone, contact the signal operator to check if is safe to cross.

▶ Tell the operator when you are clear of the crossing.

Stop sign

Direction to phone

Signals

Location of phone

Pedestrians must stop at the 'Stop' line

TO CONTACT RAILTRACK phone 020-8123-4567

Number for contacting rail operator

PARK HERE AND USE PHONE AT CROSSING

For large or slow vehicles

General rules and regulations continued

The number in brackets at the end of each question indicates how many correct answers you should mark.

49 When turning left, which of the following applies? (1)

a Don't overtake just before turning.

b Don't look in the mirrors just before turning.

c Don't look over your left shoulder.

d Don't signal your intention in good time.

50 If you want to turn left, which of the following applies? (1)

a Look out for motorcyclists on your right.

b Give way to vehicles in a reserved lane.

c Keep as close as possible to the centre of the road.

d All of these.

51 If you need to make a U-turn, when is it best to do this? (1)

a At a roundabout.

b In a quiet street.

c When the road is clear in all directions.

d All of these.

52 When entering a roundabout, what should you do? (2)

a Apply the M-S-M sequence at each stage.

b Give way to traffic approaching from your left.

c Move into the correct lane for your exit.

d Move to the centre lane as soon as possible.

53 When on a roundabout, you must: (1)

a Indicate your intention and move into the appropriate lane.

b Remain in the correct lane.

c Pass the exit before the one you need, then indicate your intention.

d All of these.

54 You approach a level crossing. What rules must you apply? (2)

a You may cross if the amber light is steady.

b Do not stop or park on the crossing.

c Cross the crossing only if there is enough space on the other side.

d An audible alarm means you still have time to cross.

55 At a controlled level crossing you must: (1)

a Stop when the red lights are flashing.

b Stop when the steady amber light is on.

c Stop behind the solid white line on the road.

d All of these.

56 Which of the following statements is incorrect in respect of level crossings? (1)

a Remain stationary as long as the red light is flashing.

b Stop if the barrier is being lowered.

c Don't zig-zag around the barriers.

d No barriers indicate that the line is not busy.

57 If you are herding a large group of animals and arrive at a level crossing, what should you do? (1)

a Move them across in small batches.

b Find an alternative route where possible.

c You can cross anyway as animals have right of way.

d Contact the station master on the phone for permission to cross.

58 How should a driver respond at a crossing without lights? (1)

a Stop when the barrier or gate begins to close.

b Use the phone to get permission to cross.

c Proceed as soon as a train has passed.

d All of these.

59 At a level crossing with user-operated railway gates, you must: (1)

a Open the gates on both sides of the barrier if the green light is on.

b Make sure that the green light is still on.

c Cross the crossing as quickly as you can.

d All of these.

60 Where there are no lights at a level crossing but there is a phone, you should: (2)

a Contact the signal operator to find out if it is safe to cross.

b Use the phone in the event of an emergency.

c Just cross and proceed on your way.

d Tell the signal operator after you have crossed.

| 49 | a | 50 | b | 51 | d | 52 | a, c | 53 | d | 54 | b, c |
| 55 | d | 56 | d | 57 | d | 58 | a | 59 | d | 60 | a, d |

17 Dealing with hazards

Coping with hazards is an important aspect of driving on a public road. A hazard is any object or action that might cause you to change speed or direction. Stationary hazards include trees, poles, road works, parked vehicles, motor vehicle entrances and junctions. Moving hazards include anything and anyone moving on or close to the road ahead, such as pedestrians, long vehicles, animals, cyclists, motorcyclists and horse-riders. In particular, you must be aware of children, elderly and disabled people, and learner and inexperienced drivers and riders.

General

- When you encounter a hazard, check in the mirrors and blind spots to see if it is safe around you.
- Signal in good time your intention to slow down or change direction.
- Obey any road signs or markings.
- Adjust your speed according to the situation.
- Position your vehicle correctly for the situation.
- Look out for motorcyclists, cyclists and pedestrians.

Pedestrian crossings

- Don't park on a pedestrian crossing.
- Don't park within the zig-zag line area.
- Don't overtake the moving vehicle nearest the crossing.
- Don't overtake a vehicle that has already stopped to give way to pedestrians.
- Don't harass pedestrians; allow them enough time to cross safely.

- Take extra care where the view of either side of the crossing is blocked by vehicles.
- Look out for pedestrians crossing between stationary vehicles.

Pedestrian crossings

You will be required to recognize the different types of pedestrian crossing and be able to respond correctly and safely according to the situation.

Things you must do

- React early to traffic light signals at controlled crossings.
- At zebra crossings, slow down and stop if somebody is waiting to cross.
- Use the M-S-M routine.
- If necessary, give the 'Stopping' arm signal.
- At pelican, puffin and toucan crossings stop if the lights are red.
- Give way to pedestrians on a pelican crossing when the amber lights are flashing.
- Give way to cyclists on a toucan crossing.
- Approach crossings at a controlled speed.
- Move off when it is safe to do so.

Some don'ts

- Don't approach a crossing too fast.

- Don't drive over a crossing when there are pedestrians waiting to cross.
- Don't stop on a crossing.
- Don't sound the horn to hurry people along.
- Don't rev the engine or edge forward to intimidate people.
- Don't overtake within the zig-zag lines.
- Don't wave pedestrians across a crossing.

Zebra crossings

- Look out for people waiting to cross. Slow down and prepare to stop if necessary.
- You *must* give way to pedestrians already on the crossing.
- Be particularly careful on wet or icy road surfaces.
- Don't wave people across, as another vehicle might be approaching. Be patient and wait.
- Look out for pedestrians entering the road diagonally from before or after the crossing.

Signal-controlled pedestrian crossings

Pelican crossings have two 'Stop/Yield' phases: a red stop light, followed by a flashing amber light. A pelican crossing that goes straight across the road is one crossing, even if there is a central island.

Puffin crossings have sensors that detect when people are crossing and will hold the waiting traffic on a red signal until pedestrians have left the road.

Toucan crossings allow pedestrians and cyclists to cross at the same time.

Toucan and *puffin* crossings have no flashing amber phase.

Driver responses

▶ Red light:
  – You must stop.

▶ Flashing amber light:
  – You must give way to pedestrians on the crossing.

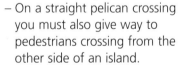

  – On a straight pelican crossing you must also give way to pedestrians crossing from the other side of an island.
  – Where there are no pedestrians on the crossing, proceed with caution.

▶ Green light:
  – Proceed cautiously, but give way to any pedestrians still crossing; be patient.

Road users requiring extra caution

▶ The most vulnerable road users are:
  – pedestrians;
  – cyclists;
  – motorcyclists;
  – horse-riders;
  – children;
  – elderly people;
  – disabled people;
  – learner drivers/riders;
  – inexperienced drivers/riders.

▶ Reduce speed and drive carefully when vulnerable road users are present.

Pedestrians

▶ Drive carefully and slowly wherever pedestrians may be encountered.

▶ The lower the speed, the less risk of killing a pedestrian.

▶ At night, look out for pedestrians wearing reflective clothing; this could indicate that an organized walk is in progress.

▶ Anticipate what pedestrians and cyclists might do.

▶ Look out for pedestrians crossing between stationary vehicles.

▶ Look out for pedestrians in crowded shopping streets and residential areas.

▶ When driving past bus and tram stops, look out for pedestrians who may suddenly enter the road.

▶ When passing parked vehicles, such as ice-cream vans, look out for children who may suddenly run into the road.

▶ You may drive across a pavement or footpath to enter a property, but give way to pedestrians and cyclists.

▶ When reversing into a side road, look around the vehicle and give way to pedestrians crossing the road.

▶ When turning into a road at a junction, give way to pedestrians crossing the road into which you are turning.

▶ Where the pavement is closed for construction, look out for pedestrians walking on the road.

Pedestrians continued

- Particularly vulnerable pedestrians are:
  - children, whose actions are unpredictable;
  - the elderly, who react slowly;
  - blind and partially sighted people (who may have a white cane or a guide dog);
  - people who are deaf (who may have a guide dog wearing a bright orange collar and lead);
  - people who are blind and also deaf (who may have a white cane with a red band, and/or a guide dog);
  - people with other disabilities, some of whom may be in wheelchairs or on powered 'scooters'.

- Reduce speed and drive carefully near schools and stationary school buses.

- Stop when instructed to do so by a school crossing patrol.

Motorcyclists and cyclists

- Motorcycles and cyclists are small and often more difficult to see than cars, buses and lorries.

- Look out for approaching motorcyclists and cyclists who may be obscured by other vehicles at junctions and roundabouts.

- Allow plenty of room when overtaking a motorcyclist or cyclist, particularly if you are driving a long vehicle or towing a trailer.

- Look out for motorcyclists looking over their shoulder, as this could indicate their intention to turn in that direction.

- Look out for motorcyclists and cyclists who:
  - may need to swerve because of road surface conditions;
  - may cut in just in front of you;
  - may pass very close to you;
  - may filter between lanes;
  - may be blown off course by strong winds or when passing large vehicles.

- Look out for cyclists crossing the road at the wrong place.

Animals

- Drive very slowly when passing animals straying, or being led or ridden, and allow plenty of room.

- Look out for straying animals where roads are unfenced.

- Be prepared to stop.

- Don't sound your horn or rev your engine near animals.

- If the road is blocked by a herd of animals, stop the vehicle and turn off your engine.

Progress test

Dealing with hazards

The number in brackets at the end of each question indicates how many correct answers you should mark.

1 Which of the following is not a general rule for dealing with hazards? (1)

a When you encounter a hazard, check in the mirrors and blind spots.

b Adjust your speed according to the situation.

c Position your vehicle according to the situation.

d Switch on the hazard warning lights.

2 Which rule does not apply at pedestrian crossings? (1)

a Don't park on a pedestrian crossing.

b Don't overtake a vehicle that has stopped at a pedestrian crossing.

c Indicate your intention to stop.

d Don't harass pedestrians on a pedestrian crossing.

3 At zebra crossings you should: (2)

a Slow down and be prepared to stop.

b Give way to pedestrians already on the crossing.

c Drive through if there are people waiting to cross as you have right of way.

d Stop only if there is a yellow light flashing.

4 How many 'Stop/Yield' phases does a pelican crossing have? (1)

a Two.

b Three.

c One.

d None of these.

5 Which statement applies to a toucan crossing? (1)

a Only pedestrians may cross.

b Pedestrians, cyclists and small motorcycles can cross.

c Pedestrians and cyclists only may cross.

d In some cases, small vehicles are permitted to use a toucan crossing.

6 Which statement is correct? (1)

a Toucan and puffin crossings have no amber phase.

b Cyclists and pedestrians must give way to each other at toucan crossings.

c A flashing amber light at a crossing means motorists may proceed.

d A green light at a crossing means you may proceed as pedestrians must give you right of way.

7 Which are considered vulnerable road users? (1)

a Pedestrians and horse-riders.

b Cyclists and motorcyclists.

c Children and the elderly.

d All of these.

8 In respect of pedestrians, which of the following applies? (1)

a The lower the speed, the less the risk of pedestrians being killed.

b At a junction, you must give way to pedestrians crossing the road into which you are turning.

c Pedestrians have right of way on a footpath.

d All of these.

9 How would you identify a blind and deaf pedestrian? (1)

a They would carry a white cane with a red band.

b They may have a dog with a bright orange collar and lead.

c They may have a guide dog.

d They have a white cane and carry a red flag.

10 When must a driver stop? (1)

a When instructed to do so by a school crossing patrol.

b When there is an altercation happening on the pavement.

c To get a better view of an accident.

d When in the wrong lane at a junction.

11 Which statements are correct? (2)

a Allow plenty of room when overtaking a motorcyclist.

b A motorcyclist may indicate an intention to turn by looking over his shoulder.

c Motorcyclists have right of way in the rain.

d Motorcyclists can hold on to other vehicles for support at a traffic light.

12 In the presence of roaming animals you should: (1)

a Sound the horn to stop them straying on to the road.

b Reduce speed and drive past them slowly.

c Stop and herd them into the nearest field.

d Pay no attention to them.

7 d	8 d	9 a	10 a	11 a, b	12 b
1 d	2 c	3 a, b	4 a	5 c	6 a

Horse-riders

▶ Regard horses as a potential hazard: drive carefully and be prepared to slow down.

▶ When passing horses and riders, slow down and allow plenty of space, because horse-riders may ride in double file. Take extra care when the riders are children.

▶ Respond to horse-riders' signals to slow down or stop.

Elderly drivers

▶ Drive carefully near elderly drivers as their reactions may be slow.

Inexperienced drivers

▶ Inexperienced drivers include learner drivers, young drivers and new drivers.

▶ Look out for 'new driver' plates or stickers which will indicate an inexperienced driver.

▶ Be especially patient and cautious near inexperienced drivers, as their driving skills may not yet be developed.

Emergency vehicles

▶ Give way to emergency vehicles that are flashing red, blue or green beacons, or headlights, or are sounding sirens. These include:
– ambulances;
– fire engines;
– police vehicles;
– bomb disposal vehicles;
– blood transfusion vehicles;
– mountain rescue vehicles;
– coastguard vehicles;
– doctors on emergency calls.

▶ If necessary, move over and stop, without endangering other road users.

Vehicles for disabled people

▶ Look out for disabled people using a small powered vehicle that may or may not have an amber flashing light.

▶ On a dual carriageway these vehicles must have a flashing amber light.

Large vehicles

▶ Be ready to stop and wait for a large vehicle, as it may move into your lane to gain extra space to turn or to avoid a hazard you cannot see.

▶ Increase your following distance behind a large vehicle, to improve your view of the road ahead and to allow the driver to see you in his or her mirrors.

Large goods vehicle rear markings

The following markings must appear at the rear of motor vehicles over 7,500 kg maximum gross weight and on trailers over 3,500 kg maximum gross weight:

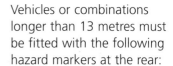

Vehicles or combinations longer than 13 metres must be fitted with the following hazard markers at the rear:

Vehicles with flashing amber lights

▶ Approach with caution when you see flashing amber lights on a vehicle. This could be a slow-moving vehicle such as a road gritter, a recovery vehicle or a vehicle that has broken down.

Buses, coaches and trams

▶ Give these vehicles priority when safe to do so.

▶ Give way to buses indicating to pull away from bus stops.

▶ A bus carrying schoolchildren will display the following sign in the front or rear window:

▶ When passing a stationary bus, coach or tram, look out for pedestrians walking into the road.

▶ Look out for buses suddenly moving out into the road or changing lanes.

Rules regarding trams

▶ Always give way to trams, and don't try to race or overtake them.

▶ Don't drive in a road, lane or other route reserved for trams.

▶ Don't park your vehicle in the way of a tram, or where it would cause other drivers to do so.

▶ At stops without platforms, don't drive between the left-hand kerb and a tram dropping off or picking up passengers.

▶ Where there is a tram platform for passengers, follow the route indicated by signs and markings.

▶ Look out for people running to catch a tram.

▶ Cyclists and motorcyclists should avoid tram tracks, or should cross them at right angles to avoid skidding, especially in wet weather.

▶ Look out for cyclists, whose narrow tyres make them most vulnerable on tram rails.

▶ Look out for tram tracks that cross the road from side to side.

▶ Remember that trams move quickly and quietly and cannot steer to avoid you.

Electric vehicles

▶ Drive cautiously near electric vehicles, such as trams and milk floats.

Road works

▶ Where you see a 'Road works ahead' sign, look out for supplementary signs giving specific instructions.

▶ Slow down and proceed cautiously.

▶ Look out for slow-moving or stationary vehicles. You may be required to stop.

▶ Don't exceed any maximum speed limit shown by a temporary sign.

▶ Use the Mirrors - Signal - Manoeuvre procedure to move into the correct lane as directed by any signs.

▶ Don't change lanes to overtake queuing traffic.

▶ Don't enter an area closed off by traffic cones.

▶ Be aware of other vehicles in the road works area, and drive carefully.

Road works on motorways and high-speed dual carriageways

▶ One or more lanes may be closed to traffic.

▶ Lower speed limits may apply, especially in contra-flow systems.

▶ Look out for 'Keep left' or 'Keep right' signs on the back of construction vehicles that may be used to close lanes for repairs.

▶ Maintain a safe following distance behind the vehicle ahead.

▶ Look out for oncoming traffic when travelling in a contra-flow system.

Hazard warning plates on vehicles

Hazardous goods

Vehicles carrying dangerous goods must display the applicable warning plate showing the hazard information.

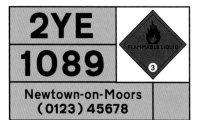

Dangerous goods in tanker (diamond indicates nature of substance carried)

The diamond symbols shown below indicate (clockwise from top):

– non-flammable compressed gas;
– spontaneously combustible substance;
– corrosive substance;
– oxidizing substance;
– toxic substance;
– radioactive substance.

Projection markers

Vehicles carrying loads that project more than 2 metres beyond the sides or rear of the vehicle must show the appropriate projection markers.

Side marker

End marker

Markings on builders' skips

A builder's skip placed in the road must be fitted with the following markers:

Dealing with hazards continued

The number in brackets at the end of each question indicates how many correct answers you should mark.

PART FOUR

13 Which response is wrong when approaching a hazard? (1)

a Check in the mirrors and blind spots. ☐

b Accelerate to get past the hazard. ☐

c Look out for motorcyclists, cyclists and pedestrians. ☐

d Position your vehicle appropriately. ☐

14 Which statement is wrong in respect of a pedestrian crossing? (1)

a You may park within the zig-zag line area but not on the crossing. ☐

b Don't overtake the moving vehicle nearest the crossing. ☐

c Don't overtake a vehicle that has already stopped to give way. ☐

d Allow pedestrians enough time to cross safely without hurry. ☐

15 What extra precautions must you take at a pedestrian crossing? (3)

a Look out for pedestrians crossing between stationary vehicles. ☐

b Signal in good time your intention to slow down or stop. ☐

c Take extra care where the view is blocked by vehicles. ☐

d Hoot to warn the pedestrians of your presence. ☐

16 Which signal-controlled crossing has a red 'Stop' light followed by a flashing amber light? (1)

a Puffin crossing. ☐

b Toucan crossing. ☐

c Pelican crossing. ☐

d Zebra crossing. ☐

17 At a flashing amber light at a pedestrian crossing: (3)

a Always stop. ☐

b Give way to pedestrians already on the crossing. ☐

c Where there are no pedestrians on the crossing, proceed with caution. ☐

d On a straight pelican crossing give way also to pedestrians crossing from the other side of the island. ☐

18 What should you do when passing parked vehicles such as ice-cream vans? (1)

a Stop to buy an ice-cream. ☐

b Signal to the vendor to move to an official vending area. ☐

c Look out for children who may suddenly run into the road. ☐

d Do nothing special. ☐

19 If you see pedestrians wearing reflective clothing at night, what might you expect? (2)

a There are a lot of traffic officers on duty in that area. ☐

b An organized walk is in progress. ☐

c Potential hazards, probably pedestrians. ☐

d Nothing in particular. ☐

20 Which of the following statements are correct? (2)

a The lower the speed, the less risk of killing a pedestrian. ☐

b Pedestrians never cross the road from between stationary vehicles. ☐

c In crowded shopping streets be particularly careful about pedestrians on the road. ☐

d Roads are for vehicles. Motorists are not responsible for silly behaviour of pedestrians. ☐

21 Flashing amber lights on a vehicle suggest that you should approach with caution because the vehicle may be: (3)

a A police vehicle. ☐

b A slow-moving vehicle. ☐

c A road gritter. ☐

d A recovery vehicle. ☐

22 Why should you increase your following distance behind a large vehicle? (2)

a To avoid noxious exhaust fumes. ☐

b To improve your view of the road ahead ☐

c To allow the driver to see you in his or her mirrors. ☐

d In case it is carrying hazardous substances. ☐

23 Which of the following statements are true? (3)

a Give buses and coaches priority when safe to do so. ☐

b Give way to a bus indicating to pull out from a bus stop. ☐

c You may drive in a road or lane reserved for trams only if it is safe to do so. ☐

d Always give way to trams. ☐

24 Where there are road works on a motorway or high-speed dual carriageway: (3)

a Maintain a safe following distance. ☐

b A contra-flow system may be in operation with oncoming traffic. ☐

c Lower speed limits may apply. ☐

d The speed limit is always reduced to 20 mph. ☐

24	a, b, c	23	a, b, d	22	b, c	21	b, c, d	20	a, c	19	b, c
18	c	17	b, c, d	16	c	15	a, b, c	14	a	13	b

18 Dealing with emergencies

Emergency situations include vehicle breakdowns, objects falling from vehicles, and accidents. Emergencies are often dangerous and can become hazards on the road. They require extra caution and may involve first aid for injured persons.

Breakdowns on the road

In the event of a breakdown:

- If possible, move your vehicle off the road.
- If your vehicle is causing an obstruction, switch on your hazard warning lights to warn other motorists.
- Place a warning triangle 45 metres (147 feet) behind your vehicle, or use other permitted warning devices.

45 m

- Don't place warning devices on a motorway.
- If it is dark, or visibility is poor, switch on your sidelights.
- Don't stand between your vehicle and oncoming traffic.

- At night or in poor visibility, don't block the view of your lights from other road users.
- After a breakdown, to re-enter the carriageway first pick up speed while on the hard shoulder before moving into a safe gap in the traffic flow.
- Look out for stationary vehicles on the hard shoulder ahead of you.

- If you are a disabled driver:
  – Remain in your vehicle.
  – Switch on the hazard warning lights.
  – Display a 'Help' pennant, or contact the emergency services by mobile or car phone and give them your location.
- If something falls on to the road from your or another vehicle, stop and retrieve it only if safe to do so, but not on a motorway.

Accidents

(See also 'Accidents on a motorway' on page 146)

- Drivers between the ages of 17 and 25 are more likely to be involved in accidents than other age groups, and most of these are caused by driver error.

- Emergency vehicles, flashing lights or sirens may indicate that there is an accident on the road ahead.
- If you come upon the scene of an accident, proceed carefully and slow down only if necessary.
- If you are involved in an accident or wish to give help:
  – Don't put yourself at risk at the scene of an accident.
  – Stop your vehicle.
  – Switch on your hazard warning lights.
- If you are the first to arrive at the scene of an accident:
  – Ensure that engines are switched off and that no one is smoking.
  – Move uninjured people away from the vehicles.

PART FOUR

– Have the emergency services called immediately.
– Don't move injured people unless they are in immediate danger from fire or explosion.
– Don't remove a motorcyclist's helmet unless absolutely necessary.
– Render first aid as necessary.
– Remain at the scene until the emergency services arrive.

Accidents involving hazardous goods

▶ Switch off the engine and do not smoke.

▶ Don't use a mobile phone near flammable loads.

▶ Keep well away from the damaged dangerous-goods vehicle.

▶ Don't try to rescue any casualties, because this could endanger your own life.

▶ When calling the emergency services, give the details shown on the vehicle's orange hazard warning plate.

Damage or injury

If you are in an accident where there is damage or injury to a person, vehicle, animal or property:

▶ Stop your vehicle.

▶ If an injured person is lying in the road, first warn other traffic by:
– displaying an advance warning signal;
– switching on hazard warning or other lights;
– any other means that does not put you at risk.

▶ Give the following information if requested, and ask the other driver/s for the same details:
– your name and address;
– the vehicle owner's name and address;
– the vehicle registration number;
– your insurance certificate details, if possible.

▶ Within 24 hours, or sooner, report this information to the police if not done at the scene of the accident, and produce your insurance certificate within 7 days.

▶ You may also be requested to produce your driving licence and MOT certificate.

Rendering first aid

▶ Injuries must always be dealt with in the 'ABC' order:
– AIRWAYS – remove any obvious obstruction in the mouth.
– BREATHING – check if the casualty is breathing, and if not, tilt the head back as far as possible and apply mouth-to-mouth resuscitation assistance (described below) until the person can breathe unaided.
– CIRCULATION and bleeding – prevent blood loss by applying pressure over any wound to maintain circulation; if necessary, raise the limb.

▶ To apply mouth-to-mouth resuscitation assistance:
– Clear the airway.
– Tilt the head back.
– Pinch the nostrils together.
– Breathe into the mouth until you see the chest rise; repeat this every 4 seconds until the casualty can breathe without help.
– Breathe gently in the case of small children.

▶ Treat for shock:
– Keep injured people warm and comfortable.
– Loosen any tight clothing.
– Avoid moving them.
– Keep them calm.
– Make sure they are not left alone.
– Reassure them constantly.

Rendering first aid continued

▶ Don't offer injured people a cigarette.

▶ Don't move injured people or give them anything to drink.

▶ Leave casualties inside the vehicle unless they are in danger.

▶ When dealing with burns:
  – Do not remove anything sticking to the burn.
  – Douse the burns with a cool liquid.

▶ An unconscious person should only be moved if they are in further danger.

▶ Don't move a person suspected to have a back injury.

Accidents and breakdowns on a railway crossing

▶ Ensure that everyone gets out of the vehicle and away from the crossing immediately.

▶ If a railway telephone is available, inform the signal operator immediately.

▶ If possible, or if the operator instructs you to, remove the vehicle from the crossing before a train arrives.

▶ If the alarm sounds, or the amber light comes on to indicate that a train is approaching, abandon the vehicle and immediately get yourself and any passengers well clear of the crossing.

Progress test

Dealing with emergencies

The number in brackets at the end of each question indicates how many correct answers you should mark.

1 Which of the following are correct? (2)

a You may not place warning triangles on a motorway.

b In a breakdown, place a warning triangle 45 metres behind your vehicle.

c If your vehicle is causing an obstruction, wave a red flag or cloth.

d It's best to stand between your vehicle and oncoming traffic.

2 What can you expect if you see an emergency vehicle or flashing lights? (1)

a A compulsory lane change ahead.

b An accident on the road ahead.

c A protest march ahead.

d Nothing significant.

3 If you are involved in an accident or wish to give help, you should: (2)

a Be prepared to put yourself at risk.

b Stop your vehicle.

c Switch on your hazard warning lights.

d Accelerate to get away from the scene.

4 Drivers of which age group are most likely to have an accident? (1)

a 17 to 21.

b 17 to 25.

c 17 to 30.

d 21 to 28.

5 If you arrive first at an accident scene, what should you do? (2)

a Ensure that the engine is switched off and no one is smoking.

b Call your family doctor.

c Wave a red flag to warn other motorists.

d Move uninjured people away from the vehicles.

6 If you arrive first at an accident scene, you should: (3)

a Have the emergency services called immediately.

b Move injured people as soon as possible.

c Not move injured people unless they are in immediate danger from fire or explosion.

d Not remove a motorcyclist's helmet unless absolutely necessary.

7 If the accident involves hazardous goods: (3)

a Switch off the engine and do not smoke.

b Call the emergency services.

c Don't use a mobile phone near flammable goods.

d Leave the scene of the accident.

8 If the accident involves hazardous goods: (3)

a Leave the rescue operations to the emergency services to handle.

b Give the details on the orange warning plate to the emergency services.

c Try to rescue any casualties while keeping children away.

d Keep well away from the damaged goods vehicle.

9 Which statements are wrong when treating for shock? (2)

a Keep injured people warm and comfortable.

b Offer the person a cigarette or some brandy.

c Leave them alone so that they stay calm.

d Reassure them constantly.

10 If your vehicle breaks down at a railway level crossing, which advice is correct? (2)

a Each person must run as far as possible from the scene.

b Get everyone clear of the vehicle and away from the crossing immediately.

c Inform the signal operator if possible.

d Ignore the signal operator and use your own judgement.

11 What should you do if the warning system indicates a train is coming while your vehicle is broken down at a level crossing? (2)

a Abandon the vehicle.

b Try to move the vehicle as quickly as possible.

c Get yourself and all passengers well clear of the crossing.

d Yell at the signal operator.

12 When dealing with skin burns, which of these actions is correct? (1)

a Don't remove anything sticking to a burn.

b Spread butter or oil on the burns.

c Strip off clothing from the burns to get them clean.

d Cover the burn with a cloth soaked in warm radiator water.

1 a,b	2 b	3 b,c	4 b	5 a,d	6 b,c	7 a,b,c	8 a,b,d	9 b,c	10 b,c	11 a,c	12 a

PART FOUR

19 Rules specific to motorways

A motorway is a multi-lane high-speed road. Because traffic travels faster on motorways than on other roads, there is less time to react; so it is necessary to have special rules for motorways, and for drivers to be more observant than normal when driving on a motorway. You should use your mirrors earlier and look much further ahead than you would on other roads.

This chapter covers the rules specific to motorways.

Not allowed on motorways

The following people, vehicles and actions are not allowed on motorways:

- pedestrians;
- holders of provisional car and motorcycle driving licences, unless exempt;
- riders of motorcycles under 50 cc;
- cyclists;
- horse-riders;
- certain slow-moving vehicles;
- vehicles carrying oversized loads, except with special permission;
- agricultural vehicles;
- most invalid carriages;
- travelling over 70 mph or the speed limited displayed;
- travelling over the maximum speed permitted for your vehicle;
- travelling in excess of the speed limit displayed;
- reversing;
- crossing the central reservation;
- driving against the traffic flow;
- driving on the hard shoulder, except in an emergency or if signs direct you to do so;
- driving in the right-hand lane on a motorway having three or more lanes (unless the left lanes are closed) if you are driving:
  – a vehicle towing a trailer;

– a goods vehicle with a maximum laden weight in excess of 7.5 tonnes;
– an eight-or-more seater passenger vehicle with a maximum laden weight in excess of 7.5 tonnes;

- using the hard shoulder for overtaking;
- stopping on the carriageway, hard shoulder, slip road, central reservation or verge, except in an emergency, or when instructed to do so by the police or an overhead flashing red light;
- picking up or setting down pedestrians, except in an emergency;
- walking, except in an emergency.

Joining/leaving a motorway

When joining a motorway:

- Give way to traffic already on the motorway.
- Use the slip road to adjust your speed so that you merge safely into the traffic flow in the left-hand lane.
- Do not cross solid white lines that separate the lanes.
- Stay in the left lane until your speed is up to the traffic speed before overtaking.

When leaving a motorway:

- Look ahead for the exit you wish to take.

- Move into the left lane well before reaching your exit.
- Signal left in good time, and adjust your speed and slow down appropriately on the slip road.
- Look out for any sharp bend on the slip road.
- If you have missed your exit, proceed to the next exit.

PART FOUR

Lane use on motorways

▶ Drive in the left-hand lane if the road ahead is clear.

▶ Slow-moving or speed-restricted vehicles must drive in the left-hand lane except to overtake.

▶ If you intend overtaking several vehicles, stay in the right-hand lane until you have overtaken all the vehicles, and then return to the left lane.

▶ Look ahead at the signs to ensure that you select the correct lane for the route you want to follow, particularly when approaching a junction.

▶ Move into the left lane well before you need to exit.

▶ Signal left in good time and slow down on the slip road if necessary.

▶ If you are in the left lane and vehicles are joining the motorway from a slip road, move to another lane if safe to do so.

Overtaking on motorways

▶ Don't overtake unless you are sure it is safe to do so, and overtake only on the right.

▶ Don't overtake on the left unless there is a queue of traffic to your right that is moving more slowly than you.

▶ Comply with standard overtaking rules, taking into account the higher speed on motorways.

▶ Judge speeds correctly. Don't weave in and out of lanes in order to overtake.

▶ Follow the Mirrors - Signal - Manoeuvre (M-S-M) procedure.

▶ Look over your shoulder into the blind spot, and check the mirrors carefully.

▶ Make sure that the lane you'll move into is clear.

▶ Signal your intention in good time and move out if safe to do so.

▶ When returning to your lane, don't cut in front of the vehicle you have just overtaken.

Breakdowns on motorways

▶ If something falls on to the road from your or another vehicle, stop at the next emergency telephone and call the police. Don't attempt to retrieve the article yourself.

▶ If your vehicle shows signs of a problem, leave the motorway at the next exit, or go to a service area.

▶ If you can't leave the motorway, then stop on the hard shoulder as far to the left as possible, and turn your steering wheel to the left.

▶ At night, you may switch off your headlights if you are on the hard shoulder.

▶ If possible, stop near an emergency telephone, because these give easy access to emergency services.

▶ If you use your mobile phone, advise your location by checking the marker posts on the left.

▶ Ensure that everyone leaves the vehicle through the left-side doors.

▶ Leave any animals inside the vehicle or, in an emergency, keep them properly controlled on the verge.

▶ Don't attempt to repair your vehicle at all.

Breakdowns on motorways continued

▶ Keep passengers away from the carriageway and the hard shoulder.

▶ Ensure that children are kept under control.

▶ Use the nearest emergency phone on your side of the carriageway to notify the police.

▶ Face oncoming traffic while using the emergency phone.

▶ Provide the police with full details of the situation, and tell them if you are a vulnerable motorist.

▶ Wait in a safe place near your vehicle.

▶ If you feel threatened by someone, get into your vehicle by a left-side door, and lock the vehicle; get out once the threat has passed.

▶ If you can't move on to the hard shoulder:
  – Stop the vehicle and switch on your hazard warning lights.
  – Get out of your vehicle only when it is safe to do so.
  – Don't set up any warning device on the carriageway.

▶ Before re-entering the carriageway, build up speed on the hard shoulder and watch for a safe gap in the traffic. Look out for any stationary vehicles on the hard shoulder.

Accidents on a motorway

(See also the section 'Accidents' on page 140)

If you are involved in an accident on a motorway, or stop to give help, follow these procedures:

▶ Immediately call the emergency services with full details.

▶ Use the emergency phone, which facilitates identifying the location of the accident.

▶ If you use another phone, have details of the correct location ready, according to the roadside marker posts.

▶ You will be asked the number of the emergency telephone, details of yourself and your vehicle, and whether you belong to a motoring organization.

▶ If possible, keep people away from traffic, the hard shoulder and the central reservation.

▶ Warn other traffic.

▶ Follow the general procedures for accidents as set out on pages 140–1.

Rules specific to motorways

The number in brackets at the end of each question indicates how many correct answers you should mark.

1 Which of the following are not allowed on a motorway? (2)

a Motorcycles under 100 cc. ☐

b Exceeding the speed limit for your class of vehicle. ☐

c Driving on the hard shoulder. ☐

d Towing a trailer. ☐

2 If no speed limit is displayed on a motorway, what is the maximum speed permitted? (1)

a 60 mph. ☐

b 70 mph. ☐

c 80 mph. ☐

d No speed limit. ☐

3 When may you drive on the hard shoulder of a motorway? (1)

a Only when overtaking a slow-moving lorry. ☐

b Only when towing a caravan. ☐

c Only in an emergency. ☐

d Never. ☐

4 When may you stop on the verge of a motorway? (2)

a When picking up pedestrians. ☐

b When instructed by the police. ☐

c In an emergency. ☐

d When instructed by an overhead flashing green light. ☐

5 To overtake several vehicles on a motorway, you should: (1)

a Return to your lane after overtaking each vehicle. ☐

b After overtaking all the vehicles, remain in the right-hand lane. ☐

c Rather not overtake as it could be dangerous. ☐

d Stay in the right-hand lane until you have overtaken all the vehicles and then return to the left lane. ☐

6 Which actions are necessary on a motorway? (3)

a Judge speeds correctly. ☐

b Use hand signals frequently. ☐

c Look well ahead at the signs. ☐

d Signal in good time before exiting or changing lane. ☐

7 On a motorway, when may you overtake on the left? (1)

a When the vehicle ahead is going slowly. ☐

b When the vehicle ahead is a lorry. ☐

c If a queue of traffic on your right is moving slower than you. ☐

d When the vehicle ahead is emitting excessive exhaust smoke. ☐

8 If something falls on to the motorway, what should you do? (2)

a Stop as soon as possible to retrieve it. ☐

b Don't attempt to retrieve it yourself. ☐

c Flash your lights to warn other motorists. ☐

d Stop at the next emergency telephone and call the police. ☐

9 If your vehicle breaks down on a motorway at night, you should: (1)

a Stop on the hard shoulder. ☐

b Stop on the central reservation. ☐

c Ensure that occupants leave the vehicle by the right-side doors. ☐

d Stop and take a nap until daybreak. ☐

10 When using an emergency phone, you should: (3)

a Give the police your mobile phone number. ☐

b Face oncoming traffic. ☐

c Give the police full details of the situation. ☐

d Tell the police if you are a vulnerable motorist. ☐

11 After calling the police about a breakdown, you should: (1)

a Get back into your vehicle and wait for the police. ☐

b Wait in a safe place near your vehicle. ☐

c Walk to the nearest motorway exit. ☐

d Phone every 5 minutes to check when they will be there. ☐

12 When calling the police about a breakdown you will be asked: (3)

a The number of the emergency telephone. ☐

b The ages of all the occupants. ☐

c Whether you belong to a motoring organization. ☐

d Details of yourself and your vehicle. ☐

12 a, c, d	11 b	10 b, c, d	9 a	8 b, d	7 c
6 a, c, d	5 d	4 b, c	3 c	2 b	1 b, c

20 Additional rules for motorcyclists

Generally, motorcycle riders and passengers are governed by the same rules that apply to other road users. However, there are some requirements that apply only to motorcyclists.

Rules for motorcyclists

- Riders and passengers on motorcycles, scooters and mopeds must wear approved protective helmets.

- Protective helmets must be securely fastened.
- Approved eye protectors, ear protection, strong boots, gloves and suitable protective clothing must be worn.

- Don't carry more than one passenger on a motorcycle.

- A pillion passenger must sit astride the proper seat.
- The passenger must keep both feet on the footrests.

To be more visible:

- In daylight, wear white or brightly coloured or fluorescent clothing or equipment.
- In daylight, ride with your headlights on dip.
- At night, wear reflective clothing or equipment.

The Hazard Perception Test

The Hazard Perception Test (HPT) follows the Theory Test and includes 14 video clips of various traffic situations. Each clip lasts about a minute, during which you must respond to each hazard as it develops by clicking a button on a computer mouse. Before you begin the HPT, you will be shown an introduction that explains how to complete the test.

There is always more than one hazard during each video clip. In order to score, you must respond to a potential hazard before it has become a real hazard, and the sooner you respond, the higher your score will be. So you will need to watch each scene very closely as the various hazards appear, in order to identify each one as soon as possible.

To prepare for this test, study the following descriptions of potential hazards, note the helpful tips that follow, and then do the 'Static Hazard Perception Test' provided.

Hazard management

Good hazard perception includes:

- scanning the road ahead;
- anticipating reactions and behaviour;
- planning your response;
- allowing enough space or time to respond; and
- selecting the appropriate speed or action for the situation.

When encountering hazards you should concentrate on the situation ahead and respond with courtesy and consideration for other road users in order to reduce any possible risks involved. As you drive, you should scan all around your vehicle and always be thinking, 'What if?' in respect of any potential hazards that you encounter. For example:

- What if that child ran out?
- What if that motorcyclist skids and falls?

You must always prioritize hazards and be ready to react accordingly. You must check for hazards in the distance, mid-ground and foreground, as well as behind and to the sides of your vehicle.

Before you react to a hazard you should apply the M-S-M routine. Check in the mirrors to establish what is happening around your vehicle; if necessary, signal your intentions and change your speed or position to accommodate the hazard.

Potential hazards

A motoring hazard is defined as 'anything that may cause a motorist to change speed or direction'. Some hazards are obvious and others are hidden. Some may require an immediate reaction while others must just be kept in mind. There are various types of hazards including static hazards and moving hazards as well as driving conditions: light, visibility, road and weather conditions. You must be on the lookout for these all the time.

Static hazards include:

- crossings;
- junctions;
- roundabouts;

- bends;
- poles;
- bridges;
- driveways;
- blind rises.

Moving hazards include:

- horses and other animals that may become startled and bolt into the road;
- pedestrians, children and old people, who may suddenly enter the road;
- cyclists and motorcyclists, who are less visible in traffic;
- cars that may be driven by inconsiderate or drunk drivers;
- large vehicles, which travel slowly and need more space for manoeuvring.

Light hazards include:

- bright sunshine and headlights that throw shadows and may cause temporary blindness;
- twilight and darkness, which obscure things and affect depth perception;
- bright tail lights and fog lights that may dazzle your vision;
- smoke from fires, which hides your view of the road ahead.

Road conditions hazards include:

▶ potholes, which can cause motorists to swerve suddenly;

▶ uneven road surfaces, which can cause motorists to lose control of their vehicles;

▶ narrow roads, which make pulling over or overtaking difficult;

▶ wet or muddy roads, which are dangerous to ride on and may cause motorists to reduce speed or direction;

▶ hidden driveways from which vehicles or animals may suddenly enter the road.

Weather conditions hazards include:

▶ rain, which increases stopping distance and decreases visibility;

▶ fog or smog, which reduce visibility;

▶ snow and ice, which make road surfaces slippery, and increase stopping distance by 10 times;

▶ windy conditions, which make driving difficult for high-sided vehicles and motorcyclists.

What to look out for

▶ Traffic signs that warn of possible danger on the road ahead, e.g:

Slow down

Road works ahead

Pedestrians ahead

Hump bridge ahead

Speed limit reduction

Narrow road ahead

Double bends ahead

▶ Hazard warning lines on the road.

▶ Parked vehicles restricting visibility, or out of which the driver may suddenly emerge, or which may pull off suddenly.

▶ Schoolchildren, elderly people, dustbins on the roadside, obscured pedestrian crossings.

▶ Cyclists and motorcyclists, slow-moving vehicles.

▶ People moving or waiting to catch a bus.

▶ Traffic entering junctions or changing lanes suddenly.

▶ The indicators, brake lights and reverse lights on vehicles ahead of you.

▶ School crossing patrols.

▶ The feet of pedestrians visible under parked vehicles: they may enter the road suddenly from the other side of the vehicle.

▶ Construction vehicles, milk floats, ice-cream vans.

▶ Oncoming vehicles in the middle of narrow roads or waiting to cross the road.

▶ Motorcyclists looking over their right shoulders wanting to turn right.

▶ Motorcyclists filtering through traffic jams or queues of traffic.

Some useful tips

▶ Concentrate on the computer screen carefully.

▶ Be ready with your finger poised to click the mouse button as soon as you perceive a potential hazard appearing.

▶ Scan the entire road situation – ahead and to the sides – and see if anything you notice could become a hazard.

▶ Some situations may not appear at first glance to be a hazard. For example, a tractor in the distance ahead may appear to be in a field, but when rounding the bend you could find that it is on the road itself.

▶ Scan, identify, interpret, predict, and respond quickly with the mouse-click.

▶ Remember, the sooner you respond correctly, the higher you will score in the test.

Static Hazard Perception Test

▶ To assist you in preparing yourself for the Hazard Perception video test, the next page gives some mock samples of the kinds of scene that might be included in the official video clip. Obviously these samples are static, whereas the real test will be a movie-video. These scenes will, however, give you a feel of what to expect.

How to do this static test

▶ Look at each picture carefully and try to identify one potential hazard in that particular scene. Once you think you've spotted the hazard, circle it with a pen or pencil and do the same for the next picture. When you've finished identifying one hazard in each of the eight pictures, turn to page 152 to check the answers against what you've circled to see how well you did.

If you missed the correct hazard, study the picture again carefully to make sure you can identify the hazard as explained on page 152.

Hazard Perception practice test

For each scene below, identify the key potential hazard and mark it with a pen or pencil. Once you've done all eight samples, turn to the next page for the correct answers.

1

2

3

4

5

6

7

8

Practice test answers

Scene 1
You should have marked the nearest vehicle on the verge.

Its reversing lights are on, indicating that the vehicle is reversing into the road, and there is a risk that the driver may not wait for oncoming traffic to pass before entering the road in front of you.

Scene 2
You should have marked the nearest vehicle in the right lane.

The road sign indicates that that the right-hand lane ends ahead. Vehicles in that lane will therefore need to slow down and move across into the lane on the left. Slow down to allow vehicles in that lane to merge into your lane. Be aware that the driver of the nearest vehicle ahead of you may not signal his intention and may cut in front of you dangerously.

Scene 3
You should have marked the lorry coming out of the side road at the junction ahead.

The driver may be waiting for the vehicle ahead of you to pass the junction before he enters the road in front of you without waiting for you to pass the junction too. This could cause a collision if you don't slow down in anticipation of such a situation arising.

Scene 4
You should have marked the left-hand bend in the road ahead.

There is no road sign to warn you of the bend ahead, so you need to be observant and looking well ahead to be aware of the potential hazards associated with a blind bend. For example, there might be pedestrians walking on the road towards you just around the bend, or a vehicle broken down on your side of the road.

Scene 5
You should have marked the road at the edge of the building on the right.

Your view to the right of the intersecting road is reduced by the building's presence so close to the road, and you cannot see whether there is any traffic approaching from the right. Similarly, any approaching traffic can't see you either. The rule is, if you can't see, then don't move. It would be best to edge your way forward very slowly until you can see whether the road is clear to cross.

Scene 6
You should have marked the red car overtaking the bus.

As there are no passengers waiting to board the bus, it is obviously already pulling away from the bus stop. The driver of the red car may decide not to give way but to move into your half of the road in order to overtake the bus. You may need to move to the left or even into the left lane which may already have a traffic flow in it, thus preventing you from doing so.

Scene 7
You should have marked the driver's door of the first car parked on the left.

The street is narrow, with cars parked on both sides. The driver is seated in the first car parked on the left and might open his door suddenly without first checking to see if it is safe to do so. You should also keep a look-out for any children or other pedestrians who might suddenly walk on to the road from between parked vehicles in narrow streets.

Scene 8
You should have marked the double-decker bus approaching the bridge.

High vehicles such as lorries and buses will probably need to move into the middle of the road in order to clear the bridge at its highest point in the arch. Anticipate this and be prepared to stop before the entrance to the bridge to allow the bus to pass under the bridge safely.

Practical Driving Test manoeuvres

This chapter shows the layouts for manoeuvres you will be required to do during the Practical Driving Test. Details of what the examiner will be watching for have already been given in earlier chapters.

Reversing around a corner

You will be asked to:

▶ position your vehicle for reversing;

▶ reverse your vehicle towards a corner;

▶ reverse around the corner into a side road;

▶ straighten up the vehicle and continue reversing for a reasonable distance;

▶ stop and wait for your examiner's next instruction.

You should do this:

▶ smoothly;

▶ correctly;

▶ safely;

▶ under full control.

For further details see page 37.

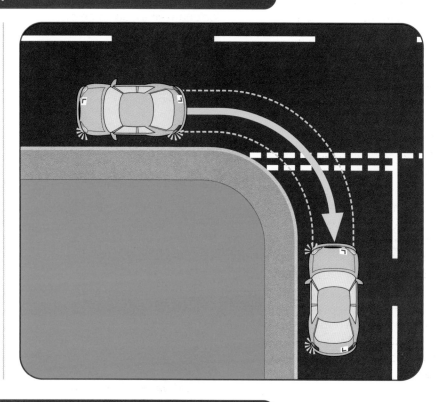

Reversing into a parking bay

You will be required to:

▶ line your vehicle up correctly and stop;

▶ reverse safely and neatly into a demarcated parking bay.

You should do this:

▶ under full control;

▶ safely and steadily;

▶ using effective all-round observation;

▶ showing due consideration to other road users.

For further details see page 117.

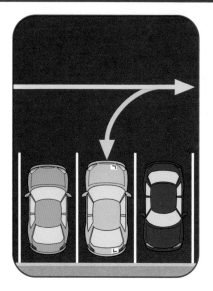 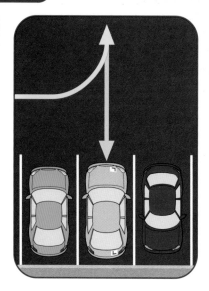

Parking behind a parked car

You will be required to:

◗ stop alongside a vehicle that is parked at the kerb with a space of about two car lengths behind it;

◗ reverse safely into the space;

◗ stop parallel and reasonably close to the kerb.

You should do this:

◗ correctly and safely;

◗ using effective all-round observation.

For further details see page 117.

Turning in the road

You will be required to:

◗ stop on the left of the road in preparation to turn your vehicle around so that it faces in the opposite direction on the other side of the road;

◗ make proper use of the forward and reverse gears, clutch, brakes and steering, which will take at least three moves;

◗ stop parallel and reasonably close to the kerb.

You should do this:

◗ smoothly and safely;

◗ using effective all-round observation.

For further details see page 127.

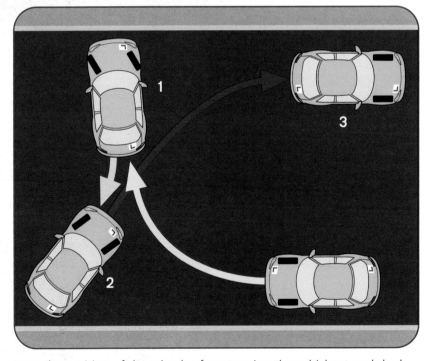

Note the position of the wheels after stopping the vehicle at each kerb.

Reversing with a trailer

If towing a trailer, you will be required to:

▶ drive the vehicle–trailer combination and stop between Cones A and A1, as shown in the layout on the right;

▶ reverse and steer at an angle so that you pass Cone B safely;

▶ steer to the opposite side so that you reverse straight between the two markers into the parking bay;

▶ stop with the rear of the trailer in the painted yellow box area at the end of the bay.

You should do this:

▶ under full control;

▶ using effective all-round observation;

▶ with good judgement of the vehicle and trailer size.

For further details see page 9.

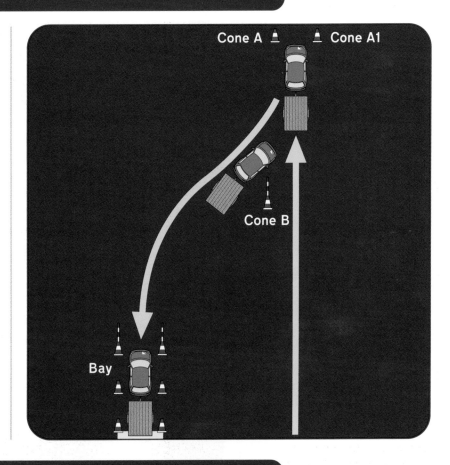

Cone A   Cone A1

Cone B

Bay

Braking and stopping with a trailer

If towing a trailer, you will be required to:

▶ drive straight ahead and accelerate to at least 20 mph until the front of your vehicle passes between two markers approximately 61 metres (200 feet) ahead;

▶ stop the vehicle and trailer as quickly as possible.

You should do this:

▶ under full control;

▶ as safely as possible;

▶ in a straight line without skidding or stalling the engine.

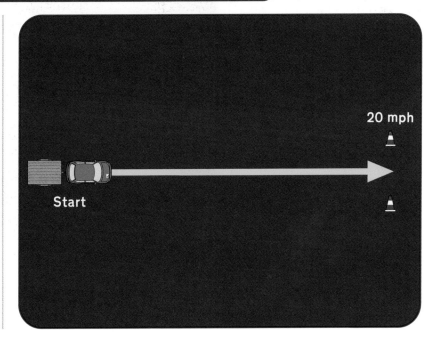

20 mph

Start

Motorcycle manoeuvres

If you're doing the motorcycle riding test you will be required to:

▶ take your motorcycle off its stand and wheel it backwards in an arc of 180°, then place it back on its stand;

▶ remove it from its stand again and start the engine to commence a series of manoeuvres.

The manoeuvres include the following:

▶ riding through a slalom of cones;

▶ performing a 'figure-of-eight' twice;

▶ negotiating a left-hand bend at 20 mph (30 kph);

▶ performing a collision avoidance manoeuvre at 30 mph (50 kph);

▶ doing a controlled stop;

▶ making a controlled U-turn;

▶ doing a slow ride taking at least 10 seconds, between two sets of cones 10 metres apart;

▶ negotiating a right-hand bend at 30 mph (50 kph);

▶ safely performing an 'emergency stop' at 30 mph (50 kph).

You should perform each manoeuvre at all times:

▶ under full control;

▶ with the appropriate use of steering, gears and brakes.

The chart to the right shows the layout of the manoeuvring course you will be required to follow, and the points at which each manoeuvre is to take place (see key on the right).

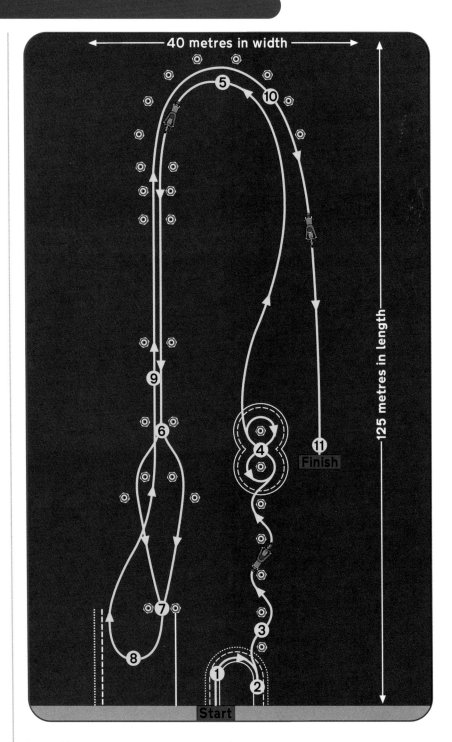

1 Off the stand and wheel the machine backwards
2 On and off the stand
3 Slalom
4 Figure-of-eight
5 20 mph (30 kph) circuit ride
6 30 mph (50 kph) circuit ride
7 Controlled stop
8 U-turn
9 Slow ride
10 20 mph (30 kph) circuit ride
11 30 mph (50 kph) emergency stop and on the stand